SPEAK
Without Fear

SPEAK
Without Fear

A Total System for
Becoming a Natural,
Confident Communicator

Ivy Naistadt

HarperResource
An Imprint of HarperCollins *Publishers*

SPEAK WITHOUT FEAR. Copyright © 2004 by Ivy Naistadt. All rights reserved. Printed in the United States of America. No part of this book may be used or reproduced in any manner whatsoever without written permission except in the case of brief quotations embodied in critical articles and reviews. For information address Harper-Collins Publishers Inc., 10 East 53rd Street, New York, NY 10022.

HarperCollins books may be purchased for educational, business, or sales promotional use. For information please write: Special Markets Department, HarperCollins Publishers Inc., 10 East 53rd Street, New York, NY 10022.

First HarperResource paperback edition published 2005.

Designed by Joy O'Meara

Library of Congress Cataloging-in-Publication Data has been applied for.

ISBN 0-06-052449-9 (pbk.)

05 06 07 08 09 WBC/RRD 10 9 8 7 6 5 4 3 2 1

To my husband, David, for your love,
patience, and endless support

CONTENTS

ACKNOWLEDGMENTS

Once in a great while you have the opportunity to accomplish something that leaves an indelible imprint on your life. Writing this book has been that experience for me. The ideas presented here gestated for many years, and when the time was right, they emerged in book form. However, a project like this doesn't happen without the guidance, talents, and influence of many other people.

With deep appreciation, I would like to thank the following people for all of their efforts and for those in my lifetime who encouraged me to speak without fear.

First I want to thank my partners in the publishing journey. I especially want to thank John McCarty for initiating this project, seeing its true potential, and encouraging me to move forward. He enthusiastically walked me through the process, and his outstanding organizational skills and talent helped me to find my own writing voice. For all of this I cannot thank him enough.

Laureen Rowland, my literary agent at the David Black Agency, who made me believe this was all possible. Her insights, sensitivity, and astute business acumen have been a gift that I will be forever grateful for. She is everything she promised to be, and anyone who has the opportunity to work with her is very fortunate indeed.

Joy Tutela, also at the David Black Agency, for her exceptional guidance and continued support. Megan Newman, editorial director at HarperCollins—thank you so much for a spectacular opportunity and such genuine enthusiasm for my work. Greg Chaput, my editor at Harper—your sensitive ear, keen eye, and unerring attention to detail guided and strengthened the entire manuscript.

. Next I want to acknowledge the invaluable advisors and mentors I have had along the way who guided, inspired, and supported me at different stages in my career. A heartfelt thank-you to Diane Winter Connors for giving me tools that lasted a lifetime. I want to thank Lara de Freitas for her professional consultations at critical stages of the writing process and confidence in this work. I am also extremely grateful to Arnold Derwin for his unending personal generosity, intelligence, humor, and perspective when it was most needed.

There have been teachers in my life whose impact has been paramount to my professional success. I am one of many who have been blessed to have been inspired by the gifted coach and speaker the late Bill Gove, and Larry Moss, an exceptional acting coach and director, whose own style informed the way I worked in the early stages of my career.

I am also extremely appreciative of the expert and sound business advice from Alan Neigher and guiding hands from the gifted Joseph Piazza and James Huelbig as well as Louise Maniscalco.

I especially want to thank my business associate and technical expert Rick Rothery for an unsurpassed sustained level of professionalism and enthusiasm that has supported my efforts since 1986. The quiet calm and expertise he brings to the mix makes every program seamless and adds tremendous value.

I want to thank a special circle of friends who shared in my excitement. My dear and talented friend Michael Leeds for his personal and professional guidance and input. Marta Sanders, Susan Mansur, Marta and Wally Ruiz, Eileen and Stephen Geiger, Ken Marino, and all of my friends in New York and Pennsylvania—a heartfelt thanks for your genuine abiding support and interest. And to the Ladies of the Lake: Hetty Baiz, Nancy Barlow, Barbara Beane, Gladys Bernet, Gloria Fassett, and Molly

Hahesy, whose kindness and friendship sustained me during the critical summer of 2002.

My following friends from NSA: Ed Brodow, Debra Burrell, Mary Bryant, Peguine Echevarria, and Richard Thieme for their professional guidance and contributions. I especially want to thank Bob Frare for his expert counsel, professional support, and friendship.

I have been privileged to work with a number of talented and dedicated professionals over the years who have supported my work, and they all have my gratitude, including John Hughes, Ken Patterson, Jeff Malley, and most recently, Irene Meader and Ray Kirk.

And, of course, I want to thank my family for their support and understanding. A special thank-you to my nephew John Wilson, whose encouragement and enthusiasm meant so much to me throughout this process. To my mother, who taught me that discipline, professionalism, and hard work pay off. To my father, the late Philip Naistadt, you are forever a part of my life. You were always driving miles to see your daughter perform, and I know you are watching today. Stay tuned!

Finally, my deepest gratitude goes to all of my clients whose own struggles and successes inspired this work and all of whom contributed to this book in more ways than they know.

INTRODUCTION
All the World's a Stage

A Funny Thing Happened on the Way to the Forum

Dynamic and effective public speaking has been a concern since the days when Demosthenes stuffed marbles in his mouth to keep from stuttering at his legions of listeners in the Parthenon. And for many working Americans today, it is a concern that has only deepened. I've seen this confirmed not only in the growth of my business but in major newspaper and magazine articles, as well.

For example, a recent edition of the *New York Times* noted, "Workplace specialists say fear of public speaking is one of the most common career-stoppers in America." According to a recent Gallup poll, *forty* percent of Americans are terrified at the thought of talking to an audience (the only thing they dread more is snakes!). The article concludes that the ability to communicate in front of a group is becoming increasingly important in our age of electronic communication, when more and more companies are placing a higher premium on face-to-face interaction.

In other words, expectations are high these days for people in virtually every career or business to communicate in as polished and persuasive a manner as the professional interviewees we see everywhere on television. The inability to do so can damage a person's personal or professional credibility and career.

For example, George, a client of mine who runs a manufacturing company headquartered in New York City, started out as an accountant, so he's completely at ease speaking to individuals or small, intimate groups. In fact, he's very dynamic in such situations. But as a successful entrepreneur, he's now required to put himself before much larger groups of people at stockholder meetings and so on. Because he lacks experience speaking to large groups, he slips into a monotone, which prevents his real dynamic self from coming through, thus reflecting badly on his credibility as a strong leader.

During a recent downturn in his business, George had to deliver an important speech to a combined gathering of almost four hundred employees and stockholders. The purpose was to shore up morale and reassure investors that the company could weather the current down market.

Using the methods I will present in this book, we explored the underlying issues relating to his uneasiness about speaking before groups, then applied some exercises to address them, making specific, targeted changes to his delivery style and reframing his message so that he'd appear more human.

The results were immediate and significant. George's speech became more focused and personal; by incorporating experiences from his accounting years and relating them to his entrepreneurship in a humorous, self-effacing, and anecdotal way, he connected with his audience on a more intimate level, as if he were speaking to each person one on one. And as his nonverbal skills (body language, eye contact, hand gestures, and so on) grew stronger, they supported rather than distracted from his delivery.

At the event itself, the audience took to George's message just as he'd hoped—because he was able to communicate his real self. He not only looked but he sounded like a person in command of a company of significance, someone whom others would want to follow.

My conclusion, drawn from working closely with hundreds of individuals with benign forms of stage fright like George's or the more extreme forms of panic and nervousness experienced by others, is that *anyone* who suffers any form of stage fright can accomplish what George did, in either a group setting or face to face.

No matter how anxious you are about going before an audience, any audience, whether it's one or a thousand; no matter how many jobs or other opportunities you have passed up, or lost, because of it, you can combat your stage fright and liberate yourself to speak without fear—that is, comfortably, confidently, compellingly—in any circumstance.

The Importance of Being Earnest

My program for overcoming stage fright and developing a style of communicating that is natural and authentic grew out of my early background as an actress on the New York stage and in television. This solution consists of identifying both the practical (e.g., lack of a skill) and the emotional (e.g., fear of being criticized) hindrances that are standing in our way and working through them. Missing from all other books and methods on public speaking, and winning friends and influencing people, this component is critical.

Look at it like putting out a fire where there is a lot of billowing smoke. Similar to nervousness, which is just a symptom of what's holding you back, the smoke is just a symptom of the fire. Aiming a hose at the smoke won't put the fire out. You need to identify the source of the fire in order to extinguish it. Without adding this critical component to the mix, no amount of tools, tips, or other how-tos for auditioning, interviewing, speechmaking, or presenting effectively will produce results that last.

How to Use This Book

Part 1 will take you through the process of determining your level of skill and anxiety. This will have an impact on how quick and easy the fix may be, because it will help expose the *why* behind your anxiety—whether it's attributable totally to a lack of experience or need of a particular skill, a deeper emotional inhibiter, or perhaps a combination of the two. I have often found in my work that even clients whose primary difficulty is lack of a particular skill may have an emotional component, however small, preventing them from getting to their next level. Therefore, whether you are just beginning to hone your speaking skills or you are a more seasoned professional, I encourage you to read part 1 carefully. Here is where you will:

- determine *all* the issues—whether skill-based and / or emotional—standing in your way of being an effective communicator
- learn techniques designed to bring any negative emotions accompanying hidden obstacles to the surface and clear them away
- visualize a new possibility for yourself and make it a reality

In part 2, you will then be taken through the process of combining your newfound freedom from whatever degree of anxiety you may have with some straightforward tools, tips, and exercises that will enable you to develop and master a technique for speaking naturally and persuasively in any circumstance.

These tools, tips, and exercises are not "one size fits all" but are adaptable to *your* level of experience and need. Just as in part 1, whether you are an absolute beginner, someone with more speaking experience who still feels apprehensive about it, or an accomplished speaker who wants to achieve even better results, you will benefit.

Sweet Smell of Success

The one-two punch of using part 1 in combination with part 2 spells the difference between a short-term solution and a long-term fix. This is a complete solution, one that will enable you to:

- understand, manage, and even be free of your stage fright
- develop a personal style of communicating that reflects who you are, with self-assurance and authority
- translate your self-worth persuasively to get that important job or promotion
- expand your skills to increase personal productivity and marketability
- improve personal health and happiness through pride of accomplishment and bolstered self-esteem
- enjoy, rather than avoid, the experience of communicating to groups or individuals
- unleash the creative process and have more fun on the job
- find your own light and let it shine

Easy to understand and to master, it is a solution that will work successfully for *you*. And, best of all, it is one that will last.

PART ONE

The Missing Link to Communicating Confidently

1

An Approach Less Taken

Down the Up Staircase

If anyone had told me when I was growing up that I'd make my living helping people overcome their fear of public speaking to become more powerful, persuasive communicators, I would have said, "You're crazy!"

But in a way, I suppose the path my life has taken was inevitable.

You see, I'm a good example of what I preach.

Picture if you will a little girl, ten years old, about four feet tall (she'd never get much taller), lugging a three-quarter-size cello that's bigger than she is into the living room of her upscale two-story suburban home. It's practice time, which goes down like vinegar. Her mother, who happens to be a professional violinist, insists (as many well-intentioned parents do) all of her children learn to play a musical instrument. However, in this case, the cello just isn't this kid's thing. Singing, dancing, and acting *are*. Heading out the door that afternoon, the mother gives the usual instructions: "Practice, or no playtime!" And with those words, she's gone.

As soon as the little girl hears her mother's car pull out of the driveway, she shoves the cello aside, springs from the chair, dashes to a closet, flings it open, and retrieves a long-handle broom.

Tucking the broom under her arm, she makes her way up the staircase that leads to the second-floor bedrooms and positions herself at the top of the landing. She is alone in the quiet house.

The orchestra in her mind begins to play, the music swells, and she gracefully begins descending the staircase with her partner, the broom, in imagined top hat and tails. Belting out the lyrics of a show tune at the top of her lungs, she has the time of her life, lost in the joy of singing.

That night, she and her mother are watching a variety show on television. The little girl, still taken with her performance that day, is enchanted by the lead vocalist of the featured singing group, whom she imagines herself to be. Her mother gets up and suddenly switches off the TV. Disappointed, the little girl asks why, and her mother replies, "Because singers look stupid with their mouths open. That's why!"

My mother, who set an extraordinary professional example, which has served me well throughout the years, couldn't have known I would eventually pursue an acting and singing career. However inadvertently, her words did have an impact on me. And while it wasn't a total showstopper, her comment simmered inside my brain, and I allowed it to linger and affect me professionally for years.

The interesting thing is, as a child, I never thought about singing from this visual perspective. I just enjoyed doing it. And yet, this seemingly benign comment, reinterpreted and internalized by me, became a critical message I would send to myself later on—creating inhibitions. As you will find out, these interpretations have tentacles that, if the messages remain unexamined, can creep into other areas of our lives.

Butterflies Are Free

The two biggest deterrents to speaking without fear are *nervousness* and *inhibitions*. They are not the same thing.

Most everyone experiences a certain amount of nervousness at the prospect of speaking to a group, pitching a new customer, or asking for a raise. Usually, these butterflies are mild and just flutter away. But those that take wing to become a crippling form of anxiety that stops us in our tracks I call *stage fright*.

This is the condition I found myself experiencing when I moved to New York City in the early 1970s to embark upon a career as an actor and singer. To learn my craft and prepare for auditions, I studied with the best acting and voice teachers in the business. They reassured me that I had talent and a fine singing voice, and was developing the technical skills to go with them.

Auditioning is difficult at best. But for me, it was an especially painful experience because of my own self-doubts and self-consciousness. You are truly being judged, the competition is fierce, and if you don't get the job, you very often have no idea why. This just adds to your insecurity. Rejection is part of the game. This is why, in addition to talent and hard work, the way you feel about yourself and the work you do is essential to your being able to keep pressing on until you achieve success.

For me, this was a constant struggle. I was continually replaying an old tape in my head—one that said that since singers look stupid with their mouths open, I must look stupid singing, too. What I've since learned is: messages sent to us in the past by significant people in our lives, whether unintentional or intentional, can leave lasting impressions . . . creating inhibitions that affect how we deal with the present. Through sheer persistence and some very good luck—both of them a must in show business—I gradually became more secure in my craft and began landing jobs off-Broadway and small parts in films and daytime soaps. But my anxiety issues persisted, even increased.

I was almost used to the fact that auditions brought on the sweats, but now they even accompanied the jobs I landed.

I recall performing a nightclub act at a premier New York City club called the Ballroom, an opportunity that offered the kind of exposure that could open a lot of doors for me.

It was opening night. There I was in my dark little dressing room a flight of stairs down from the stage, getting ready to go on, when suddenly . . .

I started feeling physically paralyzed.

When my call came, I was unable to move from my chair.

I sat there frozen, incapable of moving up the stairs.

The show's director, Harris Goldman, who'd been the company manager of the original Broadway production of *A Chorus Line* and was used to such behavior (even if he didn't understand it), came down, saw what was wrong, and tried to reassure me as he helped me up the stairs. It was a great show, I was well rehearsed, and he knew I had the ability to pull it off, he said.

He knew . . . I didn't.

As things turned out, the act went off without a hitch, and I received enthusiastic applause. However, my underlying fear squashed any enjoyment I could have gotten from the experience.

I didn't yet understand the source of this underlying fear, nor the connection it had to the way I saw myself—or judged my own performance—onstage.

Little Me

While battling performance anxiety in pursuit of a showbiz career, I often had to take odd jobs to make ends meet. One of them, which I got through word of mouth from some actor friends and media contacts, was pitching the products and services of different companies at various trade shows as a corporate spokesperson.

At the time, I didn't take this work too seriously. It helped pay the rent and gave me the flexibility to keep up with my acting and singing classes and yet still be available for auditions. It was also more fun than waitressing.

But there was something else about it that I noticed: no matter what I was called upon to do at these shows—and I had to do some pretty outrageous things, like dressing up as a Sara Lee croissant or talking to an animated puppet—my stage fright vanished. In the face of any size audience and any technical snafu, I could be absolutely fearless.

Over time, I came to understand why. Acting or singing in a musical or nightclub act is about performing—playing a part, being somebody who isn't you. But as a spokesperson, I wasn't performing, at least not in the show-business sense, though I did draw on many of the skills I'd learned as a performer. I was getting up in front of people and speaking to them as *me* (except when dressed as a croissant).

As challenging as this work often was, I got a real kick out of doing it. Being authentic—which is to say, playing myself—allowed me to relax, even cut loose, and enjoy the "show" along with everybody else. This enhanced both my credibility and persuasiveness as a spokesperson.

Very soon I was asked by the companies hiring me to give seminars on speaking without fear to their managers and staff at business conferences.

However, as I began to move into this new and uncharted career direction, a funny thing happened: my stage fright came back.

I remember exactly when it occurred. I'd been asked to speak at a gathering of IBM executives at the Opryland Hotel in Nashville, Tennessee. The morning of the event, I began to feel the cold sweats.

What am I to do? I asked myself, with creeping self-doubt and panic. Here I was, going before an audience of Fortune 100 big-wigs looking for professional expertise and guidance on speaking fearlessly, and the "pro" was breaking out in flop sweat!

Once again, I had to dig deep into my actor's toolkit to get me through. I repeated the mantra: "These people are here to *learn* from me, not see me pass out!"

I may have been exaggerating about the prospect of passing out, but that's truly how I felt. I couldn't get through the program quickly enough, or so it seemed to me, and when it was over, I couldn't wait to leave. But my assistant came up and said, "Not so fast. There's a line of people who want to meet and talk with you."

For the life of me, I couldn't imagine why. Didn't they know I'd been a basket case up there? Hadn't they seen it?

The answer was no.

My professional skills as an actor had indeed gotten me through, and I now knew they always would. But the experience had been an ordeal. I was determined to get to the bottom of why my anxiety had returned.

Sleuth

I went to every store in New York looking for a book on combating stage fright in different situations. I found books on how to speak powerfully in public and books on what makes a successful presenter, but, as far as I was concerned, this put the cart before the horse. Nothing I found explored the entire issue; nothing went deeper into *why* I was afraid and how to get beyond it.

Frustrated, I explored the territory from top to bottom on my own. I worked with experts who helped me understand how my mother's comment and other childhood experiences impacted me as an adult. I also learned that whenever confronted by a new and different type of public speaking or communication challenge, I fell into several traps by approaching the challenge as *performance*. Let me explain.

As media guru Roger Ailes points out in his book *You Are the Message*, television has raised the bar on what we expect from public speakers. We expect to sit back, relax, and be entertained by them the way we are by the professional "talking heads" on TV—in the accepted television style, which is informal, chatty, and witty. Whether we consciously realize it or not, Ailes says (and I agree with him), we compare ourselves to that standard in public speaking situations, expecting ourselves to *perform* the same way. That's the first trap I fell into.

The second trap was forgetting one of the first instructions I got from one of my first acting teachers, the actor/producer Darryl Hickman. "You have to give up the need for a positive response," he said to me about the art of auditioning. As I came to understand what he meant, I could see that he was right.

As an actor, I had to be open and vulnerable to expressing a wide array of emotions under pressure. Naturally, I yearned for a positive response from my auditioners. Hickman was telling me that I had to learn not to allow the prospect of a negative response to get in the way of doing my work. Hard as it was, that meant giving up the need for a positive response, as well.

The same lesson applies to public speaking situations. At Opryland, in front of all those IBM executives, I'd slipped and let that need for a positive response get in my way again.

On a mission to find my own style and feel secure with it, I used everything I was absorbing, and applied the discipline I'd learned as an actor/singer to developing a process of my own for combating stage fright in any situation that called for me to speak fearlessly out of my comfort zone.

Until I began giving seminars, I never realized how many others experienced a form of stage fright in their lives the way I did in mine. Having never actually discussed the problem with my fellow actors because I figured it came with the territory, I assumed it was just something I had to live with.

I was wrong.

By working through the process I'd come up with—which involved thinking strategically, having the courage to dig deep and remove what was standing in my way, channeling my energy in a positive direction, understanding how my body works under pressure, and learning how to achieve maximum effectiveness with the right kind of rehearsal—I freed myself of the stage fright that had plagued me on and off for so long.

Believing this process could work for anyone, in any walk of life, I began using it in my seminars. And as the demand for them increased, I bid an excited farewell to stage and screen without regret to pursue my new career as a professional speaker, helping others reach their highest potential as communicators—and to feel the same sense of joy and satisfaction that comes from it that I do. The book you're holding grew out of my workshops.

The Full Monty

The key to speaking without fear is exposing the core issues behind your stage fright (issues that can be different for each of us but have common denominators) and rooting them out, then developing a solid technique you can count on for creating and delivering your message.

Identifying these issues can spell the difference between combating stage fright successfully and sustaining the kind of ambient anxiety that works like a low-grade virus. It lives inside you for years, dormant, but then, given the right set of circumstances, it rears its ugly head, exploding into full-blown illness. If you allow the source of this anxiety to remain undetected, or force it underground, you keep yourself from ever being free of it.

Ilene, for example, was a striking redhead in her midthirties who worked for the advertising group of a major magazine publisher. Whenever she had to present to senior executives in her company or to customers, she'd panic inside, throw a wall up around herself, and come across as defensive, even angry. She knew her problem would limit her future in the company at best—and at worst, make it precarious. But she was ambitious and determined to get ahead. So, she came to one of my workshops seeking a remedy.

Initially, I too found Ilene to be very defensive. She interpreted most of my feedback in the workshop as criticism. She never smiled, and projected a "little girl" image with her body language that was not at all her, diminishing her power.

I put my explorer's cap on and asked if she could think of any occasion in the past when she experienced a kind of stage fright that reminded her of how she felt now. "Whatever comes to mind," I said, "even if it strikes you as seemingly unrelated."

She thought for a moment or two, then replied, "Well, I had a lisp as a child and had to have lots of speech therapy."

I remarked on how successful the therapy had been, because she spoke very clearly and was quite articulate. She explained that it was a difficult struggle. "I always felt humiliated."

"Why?" I asked.

She described how every day at school she had to get up in front of her classmates and ask to be excused to go to the trailer next door for her speech lessons. Many in the class teased her and made other unkind comments every time she did.

There it was—the important, perhaps even critical, piece of the puzzle.

Ilene was still carrying those feelings around with her, letting them affect the present. When she made a presentation to her management or to new customers (and now presented herself to us in the workshop), she emotionally recalled the anxiety she'd felt as that girl standing up in class each day to be excused for speech lessons, and her old way of dealing with it kicked in. Her defensive wall went up, and she became guarded, unable to relax and be natural.

We all saw the relief Ilene experienced just by getting this into the open and seeing its connection to her present difficulties. Almost immediately, she lost the chip on her shoulder and began radiating a new confidence. Now that she understood the *why* behind her stage fright, she could move to the next step in the process: learning how to cope with it.

She accomplished this very successfully. Even her management noticed the change; when I next spoke with her, she proudly announced she'd been promoted.

Don't get me wrong; I'm not suggesting that the core issues behind stage fright always stem from some deep psychological wound or trauma. I'm also not suggesting that rooting out these core issues is all you need to do to succeed in overcoming your stage fright. What I *am* saying is that determining the real issues at play that are holding us back from speaking without fear is, more often than not, the overlooked weapon in the communicator's arsenal, and very often the most important one.

An Approach Less Taken

To be a good communicator, you have to be authentic, which requires finding out what's stopping you from being authentic, an approach many programs on public speaking give little regard to. They focus primarily on technique—how to write and deliver a speech, for example—rather than dealing with the issue of *presen-*

tation of self. Quite often they get good results. But typically these results don't last much beyond the workshop in which they're achieved.

Acknowledging that there's more here than meets the eye by saying to yourself, "Okay, how can I improve?" or, "What's preventing me from being the best I know I can be?" or, "I don't want to live with this fear one minute longer!" and spending the time upfront to resolve the issues holding you back, you're a giant leg up on becoming the natural, confident communicator you long to be. In no time you'll see a change in your perspective and wonder, "Why didn't I do this earlier?"

The late Bill Gove, one of the foremost keynote speakers of our time and the first president of the National Speakers Association, who won every public speaking award imaginable, once said to me, "Speaking is easy. You already know how."

With that in mind, let's turn the page and be on our way.

2

What's Your Nervousness Profile?

Four Categories

In my workshops, I've discovered that people who get nervous about giving a speech, making a presentation, interviewing for a job, teaching a class, or standing up in front of a bunch of people at a Rotary club meeting—and this pretty much describes all of us—fall into general types categorized by *when* they start getting jittery.

Knowing the general type you fall into will help guide you in the direction of a solution and toward the best course of corrective action.

Read through each type to see which description you identify most strongly with. There may be more than one, because as you go on in life speaking publicly, when and why you become apprehensive may change as your experience level and expanded self-awareness increase. For example, some of my clients have told me that they used to be what I call Avoiders (people who suffer severe symptoms and are terrified at even the prospect of giving a presentation or speech because of a lack of experience and other reasons that require closer examination). But as they spoke more in public and applied the methods and tools provided in this book, they moved to another category. This will probably happen to you, too, as you move progressively closer to being able to speak without fear.

With that in mind, let's find out what type you are. Remember: this is a tool for gaining greater clarity about yourself. There is no good or bad here. So, don't judge yourself or engage in any self-recrimination.

#1   The Avoider
When: at the mere suggestion of a public speaking situation

Avoiders experience the highest degree of anxiety at the prospect of public speaking because they will move heaven and earth to stay out of the spotlight, no matter how this may damage them personally or professionally. Here's an example:

Ryan, a market analyst recently bumped up to a supervisory job in his department, came to one of my workshops for help overcoming his fear of public speaking—not because he wanted the help but because his manager insisted on it.

As a supervisor, Ryan now had to give in-person reports to top management on a regular basis. Every time his manager asked for an advance look at Ryan's presentation, Ryan replied with an evasive "I'm . . . still working on it."

This is a classic description of the highest degree of nervousness symptomatic of the Avoider.

Ryan was terrified of having to give a presentation or get up in front of people to speak. He admitted attempting to turn down his promotion, even though his analytical and managerial capabilities clearly warranted a step up the ladder, so that he could remain safely behind the scenes. He had adopted a no try/no fail attitude, and there was no way he was going to step out of that comfort zone if he could conceivably avoid it. However, his boss had forced him into a situation where he finally had to address his fear, with me.

The degree of nervousness exhibited by Avoiders is the toughest to get at because it cuts so deep. Typically, their skill at public speaking is minimal, because they've spent their lives doing everything they can to stay away from situations where such skill is needed. Preparation for them is a nightmare because they don't know how to prepare, and so they preoccupy themselves with other, often unimportant, details as a delaying tactic. In fact, it is not unusual for Avoiders to stay out of range of promotions, turn promotions down (as Ryan tried to do), or even quit their jobs to escape the possibility of being thrust into the limelight.

Avoiders also have a tough time responding to criticism. They tend to take it personally. In their eyes, to be assessed as having done a bad job at, say, making solid eye contact during their speech is to be considered a bad person. Conversely, they are extremely self-critical and tend to focus only on the potentially negative outcome of having to give a speech, make a sales pitch, or interview for a job rather than on the task before them. "I will look foolish. I will fail. I will be laughed at. I am not good at this. There is no way this is going to turn out well . . ." They heap criticism upon themselves. This catastrophic thinking becomes so pervasive that they develop a habit of giving up before they begin.

People with this degree of nervousness are always inhibited at the idea of speaking formally to a group and sometimes even one on one. Because they spend so much time living with their fear and trying to cover it up, they have great difficulty opening up and being themselves in such situations. So, flat-out avoidance, regardless of jeopardy to career or job, becomes a lifelong coping mechanism that lasts until their boss says, as in Ryan's case, or they themselves say, "Enough!"

#2   The Anticipator
When: from the moment the speaking event is scheduled

Otherwise known as the "worrier," the Anticipator takes the Boy Scout motto of Be Prepared to a whole new level. The Anticipator reminds me of the Felix Unger character played by Tony Randall in the TV version of *The Odd Couple*. Neat, fastidious, and hypochondriac, Felix worries about *everything*. One can't imagine him ever relaxing, most certainly not in a situation where he may have to give a speech or presentation. At the conference hall where the speech or presentation is to be given he'd drive the technicians crazy with his obsessively acute attention to every minute detail, the way he does his roommate.

Proceed With Caution is another motto of Anticipators. Whether their skill level is high or low, they are consumed with every aspect of their upcoming speaking engagement, presentation, or interview; this extends right up to, during, and sometimes even after the event itself. They try to work out every conceivable wrinkle, an impossible task at best.

The problem is, no matter how much they prepare, Anticipators will still worry that it's not enough, that something somewhere they should have thought of but didn't will go awry. Instead of feeling confident and relaxed in their preparation, which is one of the objectives of preparing, they tend to be uptight. And, even if they give a great speech to a thunderous ovation, or deliver a dynamic presentation, they derive no joy from it. They second-guess and Monday-night-quarterback what they could have done better. I've worked with actors like this whose preparation techniques are so thorough and airtight that they leave no room for the oxygen called spontaneity that audiences need every bit as much as they do. On the flip side, I've seen actors who, while having done their homework, come onstage confident in their preparation but also ready to go with the flow and take on whatever comes their way. A thrilling performance is often the result—maybe not perfect, perhaps, but thrilling nonetheless.

Anticipators, like Avoiders, also have a tough time with criticism because they tend to take it personally. In large part, their obsessive focus on preparation—and the anxiety that comes with it—is to avert the possibility of negative feedback at all costs. As a result, they are toughest on themselves, spending undue amounts of time coming up with the perfect paper clip for their handouts or finding that one water glass in a thousand that is perfectly shaped to fit their hand so there's no chance they'll spill a drop on themselves or their speech and look "foolish."

Unlike Avoiders, Anticipators are inhibited to an extent. Their nerves tend to tingle the closer they get to the event itself, since their overriding concern is making a mistake. At the podium, onstage, or in the interview, they adopt a "safe" delivery style because the risk factor of being too demonstrative or too exciting is too great—or because they have a superstitious feeling that if they get too cute, it'll backfire on them.

#3   The Adrenalizer
When: just before the event

My husband, David, is a bass player. Back in the mid-'80s, he was playing a benefit to save Broadway theaters, which were then being demolished at an alarming rate. As he was waiting to go on and do a number with the cast of *Dream Girls*, a hit Broadway musical at the time, he caught an odd shape out of the corner of his eye. Looking closer, David saw that it was a man leaning over a stool and hyperventilating, as if he were either about to be sick or suffering a heart attack.

As David moved toward him, the man stood up and turned, and David recognized him. It was Jason Robards, the late actor who was well known for his performance in the Eugene O'Neill drama *Long Day's Journey into Night*, a monologue from which he was scheduled to perform at the benefit.

Having apparently regained his composure, Mr. Robards looked at my husband, and David instinctively knew not to ask him if he was all right. Later, David said, Mr. Robards went on to give a powerful and moving performance at the benefit as if nothing had happened.

What Jason Robards was experiencing that night was neither illness nor symptoms of a heart attack but something he was very used to and knew how to handle: an intense rush of on-deck nervous energy caused by last-minute jitters.

Sometimes referred to as the Fight-or-Flight Syndrome, this manifestation means not necessarily that something is wrong with you, although it sure might look and feel like it, but that adrenaline is seizing control of you. Once you understand what's happening to you and learn how to manage this burst of nervous energy, you can turn it to your advantage by making it translate to a more forceful, compelling performance.

I once saw heavyweight boxing champion George Foreman interviewed on *The Charlie Rose Show*. Rose asked Mr. Foreman if he ever got nervous before a fight. Suddenly, this big tough guy started to look a little wobbly as he responded, "Yeah. When I'm making my way from the locker room to the ring and I get to the stairs, my knees are shaking so much I just want to grab them!"

These two examples describe the range of nervousness experienced by people whom I call Adrenalizers.

Generally, the skill level of Adrenalizers is very high. They know how to prepare consistently and build momentum toward the event, increasing their preparation as the event draws nearer. They understand that the surge of adrenaline that overtakes them when they're on deck is the result of a buildup of tension from their days, weeks, or months of preparation and anticipation; they recognize and acknowledge that it comes with the territory and is a product of their excitement, rather than fear. Because Adrenal-

izers tend to have solid skills and technique and know how to prepare well, they generally have no fear of being criticized. In fact,
they often welcome an objective viewpoint and solicit criticism,
which they see as feedback that will enhance their overall performance. They also know how to take the criticism they receive. In
other words, they are able to distinguish between criticism that is
sound, accurate, and aimed at being helpful and criticism that is
negative for its own sake.

Adrenalizers must manage their on-deck nervousness with
techniques such as breathing exercises that become part of their
process in controlling the outcome of their performance. How
well they manage it affects how fluid, grounded, or centered they
will feel and, therefore, come across to their audience.

A totally uncontrolled release of on-deck nervous energy typically expresses itself in behavioral tics that distract an audience
from getting the message, no matter how credible you seem. For
example, I once saw an Adrenalizer who continually rocked back
and forth on his feet during his forty-five-minute speech until all
of us in the audience felt motion-sick.

#4   The Improviser
When: during the actual event

When I ask Improvisers how they like to prepare for an interview,
give a speech, or make a presentation, the common refrain is,
"Oh, I don't prepare. I like to wing it. I like to come across as
spontaneous." They mistake the kind of preparation that allows
you to be spontaneous with a free-flowing stream of conscious-
ness that screams at your audience: "I'm a disorganized mess!"

An architect I worked with on improving his presentation skills
is a good example. Befitting his profession, he's a visually oriented
person. Recognized and well respected throughout the industry
for his creativity, he was made president of a growing architec-
tural firm. His process of pitching ideas in the past had always

been to let his drawings speak for themselves. He believed this same process was, or should be, sufficient for gaining commitments from clients even now as president. Because of this, he felt any form of structuring his presentations to those clients would interfere with his creative flow, making him feel and sound stilted. However, he did express one of his concerns with me. He wanted to know why he would occasionally find himself uncharacteristically jittery during an actual presentation.

In a demo presentation he gave me, I witnessed the behavior firsthand. He proceeded to get more and more nervous as he went on. He fumbled with his papers and came across as not knowing where he was in the presentation or what should come next. Because he was improvising totally, thereby having no structure to build on, he seemed less spontaneous than confused, unsure of himself, and lacking credibility—as if he were making the whole thing up as he went along.

Improvisers tend to think, "Hey, Robin Williams just gets up and does it; so can I!" Well, Robin Williams doesn't just "get up and do it." As most professional comedians do, he tries out all of his material, including many of his so-called ad-libs, in a variety of venues prior to trotting it out publicly. This provides him a framework within which he gives himself room to move around and improvise safely, which he does brilliantly.

Improvising, or winging it, on the spot foments an anxiety that keeps building the more you improvise until, in some cases, an underlying insecurity develops that is so strong your nervousness type shifts from the Improviser column to the Avoider column.

Because Improvisers spend more time on the concept than the content of their communication, they mostly succeed in trying their audience's patience, even if now and again they do get lucky and succeed in putting one of their ideas across.

As far as being open to criticism is concerned, when Improvisers atypically do succeed in having their ideas understood and well received by an audience, they tend to fly high. Met with disapproval, however, they feel misunderstood or hurt, and may shut down their openness to any suggestions for improvement entirely.

Improvisers generally have a very positive outlook as to how their speech or interview will turn out. They are typically bereft of any anticipatory or on-deck anxiety, which is precisely how they can be so last-minute. They feel they have great ideas (which they may) and just want to share them. The problem is that their lack of preparation sets them up for rejection because they will most likely be sharing their ideas prematurely. They need to shift the focus of that positive attitude more to organizing and presenting their ideas (even if developing a structural process strikes them as tedious work) in order to ensure a successful outcome.

Striking the right balance between no structure and a suffocating one is, for Improvisers, the key.

As noted in the introduction and at the beginning of this chapter, knowing your nervousness profile gives you an indication of whether the solution to your problem might be a relatively easy fix—as is often the case with Improvisers and Adrenalizers—or a more complex one because it is rooted in an emotional issue that must be exposed and resolved, as is often the case with Anticipators and, especially, Avoiders.

Most of the time, I find that to different degrees, all four types may require both kinds of fixes. Even an Improviser, part of whose difficulty is probably lack of knowing how to prepare properly, may also have a deeper, more emotional component, however small, working against him or her. My extensive experience working with hundreds of people has taught me never to assume that simply acquiring or refining a particular skill will mean that all is immediately and always well.

Using what you've learned about yourself so far as a guide to determining your nervousness profile, let's now examine the kinds of obstacles that contribute to or cause the anxiety holding you back, so that you can point yourself toward a solution.

Who You Are at a Glance

Avoiders—have so much anxiety associated with speaking or communicating in any formal setting that they will go to almost any length to avoid being put in a situation that demands it. May even give up promotions or pass up job opportunities to avoid the spotlight.

Anticipators—start getting nervous as soon as they hear a speech, presentation, or a job interview is scheduled. The event could be three weeks or three months away, it doesn't matter. They will spend all of their waking time until then worrying about what can, may, or will occur.

Adrenalizers—become nervous just before the event and are suddenly hit with a surge of energy that must be dealt with, like a track star gearing up for a race who controls the surge of excess energy with focusing techniques as a way of getting ready to meet the challenge ahead.

Improvisers—get nervous during the event because they are the last-minute type who either put off preparing or spend no time preparing, then typically run into all kinds of trouble that might easily have been avoided with even just a little preparation.

3

Surface Obstacles:
the Easy Fixes

Stage fright affects millions of us each day all across the country—
in corporate boardrooms and conference rooms, in convention
halls and courtrooms, at sales meetings, on radio and TV—forcing
us into making choices that severely limit us personally and professionally.

What fuels the stage fright we experience in situations where
we're called upon to put ourselves on the line before a group or a
person is:

1. Myths about public speaking pervading society at large that
   we have bought into. We can eliminate these obstacles easily
   and quickly simply by dispelling them.
2. Skill-related roadblocks, which require a bit more time and
   effort to remove because they require learning or honing a
   particular skill. But at least the fix is clear-cut.
3. Inhibitions that plague us on an individual basis, requiring a
   deeper level of commitment to resolve because they stem
   from fears we've nurtured as obstacles over time.

Recognizing and identifying what fuels your particular form (and degree) of stage fright so that you can move beyond or even overcome it is *essential* to being an effective communicator.

This chapter focuses on the surface obstacles (the myths and the skill-related roadblocks) that cause us difficulty, which are the easiest to fix.

Let's start with the myths that hold us back.

Myths Holding Us Back

There are widespread myths about public speaking that shape our attitudes about what it takes to be an effective speaker. These myths have the poisonous effect of stopping us in our tracks from the get-go because they sell the idea that we're lacking what's "needed" to become a powerful and persuasive communicator. By accepting them as true, we allow ourselves to become convinced from the start that we're bound to fail.

By examining these myths about public speaking and seeing how and why we let them stand in our way, we can get past them. I call these myths the surface obstacles because, unlike the deeper type of inhibitions I'll explore in the next chapter, they operate on a superficial level. This makes them the easiest obstacles to remove because, quite simply, they have little or no weight at all.

Here are the most common myths about public speaking I've identified in my seminars and individual coaching sessions over the years. Let's separate fact from fiction:

Myth #1: "Nervousness Is a Sign of Weakness."

Many people genuinely believe that if they get nervous speaking in public or at an interview, this characterizes them as weaklings. So, weeks before they have to make a presentation or go for that interview, they wake up each night with the sweats, having a panic attack at the prospect of being found out they suffer from the jitters and will be seen by their employers, coworkers, and customers as not measuring up. Thus, their jitters are compounded by shame.

The truth is, most of the people I work with—even, perhaps especially, those at the highest levels of their profession—get a little tense in public speaking or interview situations. Professional speakers and performers who make their living in front of audiences get the jitters, too. In fact, if they don't get them, they get nervous about not getting them!

No matter who you are, when you're in a situation where you're putting yourself out there—on the line, as it were—you realize there is a chance you'll be rejected. So, you get nervous. That's a normal response. It doesn't mean you're a weenie. What you do with that nervous energy is what's important.

I recently had the pleasure of meeting the Tony Award–winning actress Chita Rivera. She is in remarkable physical shape and exudes the energy and charisma that make her a Broadway legend. I asked her if she was still performing. In fact, she told me, she was preparing to go into rehearsal very soon for a new play and was very excited about it.

I remarked how wonderful it was that even now, at this stage in her professional life, she could still look forward with such enthusiasm to the idea of performing before an audience. At which point, she raised her arms, clenched her fists, and said, "Yes. But I get *s-o-o-o nervous*!"

Imagine that. Here's a professional actress, a Broadway superstar, in fact, who has more than a half-century of experience performing night after night before Broadway audiences (a very tough crowd!), and she admits that she still gets the heebie-jeebies at the prospect of going out there onstage.

Others like the late actor Sir Laurence Olivier, singers Barbra Streisand and Carly Simon, actress Kim Basinger, and NBC *Today* show weatherman Willard Scott also have admitted experiencing severe bouts of performance anxiety in their professional lives. If that means they're weenies, then, hey, the rest of us might as well pack up our speeches and presentations and job applications and go home!

Nervousness is *not* a sign of weakness! It is a sign of *excess energy* that you must learn to control and redirect. When you come to understand in part 2

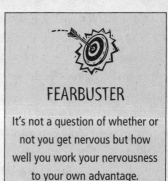

FEARBUSTER

It's not a question of whether or not you get nervous but how well you work your nervousness to your own advantage.

how your mind and body function under pressure, I will provide you with techniques for releasing stress-related energy and channeling the nervousness it produces in a positive direction that works for not against you.

This is what well-known battlers against performance anxiety have learned to do. They see their oncoming bout of nervousness, annoying though it may be, as a signal that they are getting ready to meet a challenge, and they use that awareness and their energy as fuel to do their best.

Myth #2: "You Have to Be Perfect."

Do you know people in your life who must do everything perfectly? In both their professional and personal lives, they find it necessary to cross every *t* and dot every *i* that life presents. In psychology circles, these people are known as perfectionists. While we tend to appreciate and associate hard work, responsibility, and ambition with these high-achieving individuals, there is a downside. Oftentimes they set standards that are too high for themselves, and if they fail to meet those unrealistic expectations or fall short of their goals, they are very hard on themselves.

It's also difficult, sometimes, to relate to perfectionists, because most of us are not perfect!

It's the same in public speaking, presentation, or interview situations. When I see someone who is too polished, too precise, too slick, who never makes a mistake or a misstep, my immediate reaction to them is that they're too good to be true. In other words, I don't believe them because they're just too . . . well, perfect.

What I want from a speaker, presenter, or interviewee—and I'm sure you do, too—is someone who shows up prepared, of course, but who comes across as a human being. I want a person who is capable of handling the situation—especially if something unplanned occurs, as it always does—with grace, perspective, and a healthy sense of humor.

The fact is, the best speakers and presenters rely on their willingness to be *imperfect* in order to put themselves and their messages across more effectively. They know they can't afford to be perfect because perfection doesn't exist; the unexpected will occur, and they must be free to let themselves go so they can respond to such situations.

I've experienced many such moments in my professional life. At first they were scary, but then I came to appreciate what they were telling me, which is that to aim for perfection as a speaker or presenter puts you in a tight box with no room for spontaneity and only adds to your nervousness.

Whenever I run into clients who get terribly distraught prior to facing their particular public, who start obsessing over minor details and develop an almost chronic sense of self-doubt that virtually (sometimes completely) paralyzes them, I know what arena we're in. Because of the belief they've imposed on themselves that they have to do this perfectly, they work themselves into such a state that they make the process of giving that speech, making that presentation, or going for that interview more difficult and pressure filled than it should be. By setting the bar so high for themselves (or anyone, frankly), quite often they become such nervous wrecks that they may opt out entirely.

Clearly, "I must be perfect" is an unrealistic attitude that takes you to but one destination in your personal or professional life: nowhere. I remember reading columnist Anna Quindlen's commencement address to the graduating students of Mount Holyoke College in 1999. In it, she encouraged her accomplished, hopeful listeners to give up the need for perfection in their lives as she had done in hers. "Eventually, being perfect day after day, year after year became like carrying a backpack filled with bricks on my back," she said of her early years as a student at Barnard College. "And, oh, how I secretly longed to lay that burden down."

That sums it up just about . . . perfectly.

Myth #3:   "It's a Talent You Have to Be Born with."

I'm not sure where this notion stems from—except, perhaps, that because the world's great speakers make it look so easy, the assumption is it must come naturally to them.

That is absolutely not true.

Great communicators like John F. Kennedy, Martin Luther King Jr., Ronald Reagan, and Bill Clinton—to name only a few— spent years developing and honing the Art of Speaking. (Reagan, in fact, was a sportscaster, actor, and corporate spokesperson before entering politics; so, a lot of training and practice went into his becoming a great communicator.) Furthermore, they all had, and still have in some cases, professional speechwriters working for them, whereas most of us have the additional responsibility of coming up with our own material on top of delivering it.

The truth is, 50 percent of the people I work with who find themselves in the position of having to give a speech or make a presentation have had little or no previous experience doing so. Under these circumstances, they can't expect to be polished pros like a Reagan or a Clinton, for whom communicating ideas and persuading others was and is an integral part of their professional life.

I won't argue that many good speakers do have natural proclivities in that direction. Perhaps they simply feel more relaxed and comfortable speaking before groups (although this, too, can be developed, particularly over time and with repetition). However, without a solid technique to support them, and constant application of that technique, they would not be nearly as effective, no matter how at ease they feel before an audience.

My belief is that great communicators are made, not born. And any of us can become one if we combine a real desire to achieve that goal with technique and discipline.

Myth #4:   "You Have to Be a Comedian."

There really should be warning labels on the backs of professional stand-up comics like Jerry Seinfeld and Jay Leno that read: "Don't try this at home." Or, perhaps, more to the point: *"Only* try this at home."

There is no question that making your audience laugh is an asset as a presenter or speaker, or even when interviewing for a job or college. But you don't have to be a stand-up comic to accomplish this.

Even if you can't tell a joke worth a dime and always ruin a punch line, you, too, can bring a sense of humor to your speech, presentation, or Q&A and connect with your audience. You won't have to put on funny hats or juggle bowling balls to get a laugh. Consider the great public speakers I've mentioned in this chapter. They can succeed in drawing a laugh out of us without trying to be Robin Williams. The secret to drawing laughs is to learn and practice the principles of good storytelling, which I'll cover in greater detail in part 2. These speakers enliven their words with anecdotes and stories drawn from their own experiences, which elicit chuckles of recognition from us because we can relate to them. In other words, good speakers engage us in sharing a laugh with them (often at their own expense).

Myth #5:   "Everything You Say Must Be Important."

Who among us speaks pearls of wisdom all the time? Even philoso-
phers take a verbal vacation once in a while. But a lot of what you
have to say is very important — particularly if you are selling yourself or your company, or sharing your expertise or an idea.

I've found that people who accept this myth and believe that
what they have to say is unimportant were typically brought up
with the axiom "Children should be seen and not heard." Dispelling this myth is usually sufficient to release its hold.

Myth #6:   "My Nervousness Is Worse
than Anybody Else's."

If this were true, then fear of snakes would rank higher on the list
of people's phobias than fear of public speaking!

Nevertheless, I understand where people who have this attitude are coming from. In many ways it mirrors the psychology of
a soldier who thinks that he's the only one who is scared of going
into battle, and is worried that he might be branded a coward if
his fear were exposed.

I've experienced cases of nerves at many different stages of my
professional life, and I closely guarded that secret for years, fear-
ing that if it were found out, I might not get the job — or, worse, be
seen as someone with "issues."

It wasn't until I began coaching people, particularly corporate
executives, to speak freely that I found out how truly unremark-
able my own bouts of nervousness were. These highly accomplished, successful people were concealing the same secret and
suffering the same way I was.

Some people are better able to hide their feelings of anxiety
than others, or at least they have learned how to channel their
nervousness and manage it so that it won't get the best of them

(this is me). But in order to do that you must first admit that the problem exists and not adopt the attitude that you're a lone sufferer who must always keep your anxiety under wraps.

At one point in my career I was hired to coach a group of executives to appear on a television station. Their company had created an in-house state-of-the-art studio to produce business news and information programs for broadcast throughout corporate headquarters to employees during the course of the business day. The executives were to be the on-camera talent, or news anchors.

Each admitted to me the state of panic he or she was in. And why wouldn't they feel panicky? "Anchor person" was never a part of their job description. It was like being a cameraperson who is suddenly thrust into the spotlight to fill in for Tom Brokaw.

One of these executives, a woman, told me—insisted, rather— that time was at a premium in her particular job, and so I was to teach her everything she needed to know in one session. Initially, I was taken aback. But then I realized what was actually going on with her. She was used to coping with time sheets and management reports. Now, she was coping with a serious case of performance anxiety and didn't know how to handle it. To make matters worse, she expected herself to be able to just get through it.

I suspected she felt that if her colleagues knew she was so beside herself with anxiety, they would lose respect for her as that tough cookie she'd always presented herself as being, and declare her a fraud. In truth, her nervous feelings were no different from, and no worse than, those of her fellow anchors-in-training.

Myth #7:   "It's Too Daunting and Overwhelming a Task."

Remember when you learned how to ride a bike? In my case, as I watched the older kids on my block zooming up and down the street, I kept thinking, "How will I *ever* be able to do that?"

Then one day my father took me outside and walked me through the process of balancing myself, working the handlebars, the pedals, the brakes, and so on step by step—and before I knew it, I was riding up and down that street with the older kids, too, having the time of my life.

I couldn't believe how quickly I'd accomplished this and how natural riding a bike felt to me now. I no longer had to think about how to do it; I just did it! I climbed on, and off I went.

Public speaking is similar. Suddenly you're told you have to give a presentation to senior management or deliver a speech to the Rotary club. Your brain goes into overdrive. You feel over-whelmed. You think, "It's impossible!" and you begin to panic. Pretty soon, you just want to go home, dive into bed, and pull the covers over your head. I've been there myself many times.

If that scenario sounds familiar to you, take solace in the fact that public speaking in all its varieties—from speaking before the board to the all-important job interview—is no more difficult to learn than riding a bike. All you need is a system—a place to start and a process to follow.

Part 2 of this book provides you with the basics, as well as some more advanced tips for taking it up a notch. By applying the principles and adapting them to your own needs, you'll be up and riding in no time.

Myth #8:   "You Have to Be Outgoing to Engage an Audience."

One of my clients works as a researcher in the financial sector. He's a behind-the-scenes-type guy who gathers information to help improve his company's marketing position. Typically, he shares his findings with top senior-level management, either one on one or in small meetings. But now he was being asked to pre-sent his research to the bank's sales force at an upcoming confer-ence, and he was completely rattled.

"I'm no rah-rah sales guy," he told me. "I'm not even extro-verted." He was right.

I made the point that he didn't have to be outgoing; he had to be relevant. That is to say, he didn't need a personality makeover in the image of a Tony Robbins to grab and hold his audience. What he needed was to understand his audience's perspective so that he'd present his information in a way that would be of value *to that audience*. Accomplish this, I told him, and all else would follow; he would become more energized in his delivery because his audience would actually be listening to him.

I've seen great speakers and presenters with a forceful delivery style leave audiences shaking their heads wondering, "What does all that mean for me?" I've also seen people with mediocre, even sleep-inducing, speaking styles wow an audience because of the content of their words and the relevance of their opinions. Former secretary of state Henry Kissinger comes to mind. There's no speaker in the world whose delivery style is so deadly. It's like watching the paint dry. But we listen to Kissinger because of the relevance of his opinions on the national and international scene; we want to hear what he has to say.

After making this point to my client, I set about working with him to improve his mechanics, such as watching the flow of his presentation and limiting the amount of detail he would include in his message so that it would be easier for his audience of sales folks (not analysts like himself) to digest and take away. And on the big day, he did very, very well.

Myth #9: "It's All Over if You Make a Mistake."

There will be times in your personal and professional life when you'll lose your place in a speech or presentation and won't know where to go next. Or, your mind will suddenly go on vacation in the middle of a Q&A session, and you won't know what to say. In chapter 6, I'll delve into the reasons why such mishaps occur and how to plan for them so you'll bounce back with aplomb without anyone (but you) being the wiser. For now, just keep in mind that *everybody* makes a slipup in a public address or Q&A now and then, or even more frequently. They range from experienced speakers like the president of the United States giving the State of the Union address, to college grads going for their first important job interview.

Disregard the prevailing attitude that the only alternative is public humiliation and death. Stay calm. Don't panic. And remember this: if you don't make a big deal out of it, no one else will either.

■ ■ ■

By now you should have a clearer perspective on why these myths stand in our way, preventing us from being effective communicators, and why they are simply not true.

Once you recognize you have adopted erroneous beliefs, you should begin to experience immediate relief. These false notions we pick up along the way must be dispelled because, however we adopted these concepts, whether having read them somewhere or heard them in passing, these are false myths that have shaped our current perceptions and are not reality.

You may have other myths of your own, and I invite you to question your concepts and determine if they are fact or fiction.

Now let's turn to the second category of surface obstacles that get in our way, the skill-related roadblocks, which are also easy to fix.

Skill-related Roadblocks

Unlike myths, these surface obstacles are real. But it's their very reality that makes them almost as easy to overcome as myths. You see, they stem from problems that are easily recognizable—in this case, lack of a particular skill (or set of skills). The easy solution, therefore, is to acquire that skill or skills. Of course, this solution takes a bit more effort to execute than simply dispelling a myth, but the actions required are concrete and easily mastered (depending, of course, upon how much time and effort you devote—because, as with acquiring any skill, you will get out of it only what you put in).

Lack of Communication/Presentation Skills

Ever heard of "The Peter Principle"? It was named after the late Dr. Laurence J. Peter, a teacher of business at the University of Southern California. Fundamentally, Dr. Peter's principle comes down to this: whenever someone in an organization, public or private, becomes extremely proficient at his or her job, the odds are that person will get promoted to a bigger job with different responsibilities demanding skills and expertise the person does not have. In other words, Dr. Peter says, sooner or later, everyone gets raised to his or her level of incompetence (i.e., lack of proficiency).

Dr. Peter's theorem is truer today than ever as companies increasingly require workers to do more with less and to multitask in different, often highly divergent, areas of the business because of the constraints of downsizing and stiff global competition. As a result, a financial whiz whose expertise is numbers and not people may suddenly be upped to CEO. An efficient factory floor worker may be thrust into the role of manager. Or a secretary may have to take on the responsibilities of a customer relations representative. As a consequence, each will suddenly have to communicate on a different level to a broader, potentially unfamiliar audience, via speeches, presentations, sales pitches, video demonstrations, conference calls, and so on. Since they haven't been taught the required skills or had a process for developing these skills on their own, their performance more often than not falls well below their employers' expectations. Their public words lack persuasiveness and credibility. Their self-confidence erodes. And so they do what comes naturally: they get nervous (rightfully so) and develop their own particular case of fear and loathing at the podium.

Fortunately, fear of public speaking due to lack of skill is among the difficulties easiest to overcome. All you have to do is acquire the skill(s) you lack, then work on it, adapting it to your own style, until it becomes almost second nature to you.

I learned a lot about this fear during my years as an aspiring actress auditioning for parts on Broadway. It was a heady time, coming to New York City and auditioning for parts on the legendary stages where the likes of *A Chorus Line*, *Evita*, and *42nd Street* were playing. That was my dream—to be on those stages—all the while I was a little girl growing up in Syracuse, New York. And now, here I was.

One particular audition still stands out. I was one of five actresses called back for this particular role. At first I was very excited to be called back, but as the auditions became progressively harder and more demanding, my excitement turned to fear.

At the first audition, I was asked to demonstrate my singing skills, and that went rather well. At the second audition, I had to act, and that too went well. But now I was being called back to show how skillfully I could dance, and to be honest, my dancing skills were . . . well, a bit light. In the world of the theater, there's a category for people like me: we're known as singers who move well.

I could dance, but I wasn't a trained dancer of the type you would find in the cast of *A Chorus Line* or *Chicago*, those tall gazelles who could touch their heels to the top of their heads and twist themselves into pretzels. I could touch my toes.

Well, at this final audition, the five of us were lined up onstage, and a tall—I do mean *tall* (as in six feet, seven inches)—man stepped before us. He was the show's choreographer and director, Tommy Tune. I thought I would faint, because I could only imagine what we were going to be asked to do by such a legendary taskmaster. Maybe I could hide behind one of the gazelles, I thought, and no one would notice!

There was no way out of this one. In a very soft voice with a slight Texas twang, he instructed us that when he gave us the cue, we were each to make our way across the stage, one after the other, doing what is known in dance circles as a grand jeté.

For those of you who are unfamiliar with a grand jeté (as was I), let me see if I can describe it to you. You leap several times with your legs spread wide like an open pair of scissors, landing gracefully on your feet, Baryshnikov style, each time until you've made your way successfully across the stage. As far as I was concerned, the choreographer's instructions might as well have been, "Speak your lines in Chinese, then fly."

I distinctly remember one of the fifteen producers watching the audition turn to another and whisper, "Keep your eye on the little one [me]; she's good." And my thoughts were, "No, please, *don't* keep your eyes on the little one; keep them on the big ones, the gazelles!" I felt like I was in a Woody Allen movie, and here comes the scene: Lights . . . Action . . . *Splat*!

I was going to be humiliated, and there was nothing I could do about it. But it was too late to back out now.

"Okay, ladies, begin," said Tommy Tune. One by one, the gazelles made their way across the floor, leaping—*flying*— through the air. Then it was my turn.

My mind and heart were racing. I had to do something. But what? On the spot, I came up with a brand-new form of grand jeté. There would be no leaps, no spread-eagle jumps, not even any little bunny hops from me. I sidestepped my way across the stage, like a crab on Prozac, arms flailing, desperately trying to smile through clenched teeth until I finally reached the far side of the stage (I knew I'd reached it because I practically crashed into the wall).

Well, you could have heard a pin drop. I looked out and saw fifteen horrified faces looking back at me with their mouths open, and one very tall shocked Texan in front of me, who then proceeded to politely give me the classic showbiz dismissal of: "Thank you. *Nexxxxxt!*"

What I learned from this incident was invaluable; it determined me never to be caught in a fix like that again. Although I had no ambition to become a professional dancer, I knew I needed to go back and take as much dance training as I could so that I would be able to at least get by. This was the big league, and if I wanted to be successful, I had to learn how to play the game. So, I took dance classes every day, sometimes several each day, to become proficient enough so that the next time I auditioned for a part that required me to appear dancerlike, I would get the job!

Language Barriers

If you are not yet fluent in the language of your prospective audience, or if you have a distinctive accent from growing up in a different part of the country or a foreign land, it's natural to feel a bit self-conscious and, thus, develop a case of the jitters.

Your nervousness is a well-founded reaction, because audiences do size up a speaker's intelligence, background, and level of education by observing his or her command of the language. Think of the public perception of President Bush's smarts underlying many of the jokes we get from David Letterman and Jay Leno about the president's difficulties with the English language. It's human nature to make such judgments, justified or not.

The important thing is to understand, and to believe, that you are doing your best at the time—and to acknowledge the certainty that you will get even better if you keep working at it. Don't fall into the trap of becoming so self-critical that you make yourself feel that no matter what you do, a language barrier will always be there.

For example, I have a client who is Chinese. He came to one of

my seminars because he felt his heavy accent was holding him
back from his goal of becoming a lecturer on the public speaking
circuit, like me. I gave him my professional opinion that his heavy
accent was not the overriding obstacle; it was his speed of delivery. He spoke too quickly (as do most speakers when they are
nervous, whether they have a language barrier or not). This made
him difficult to understand.

If he could learn to tell himself to slow down and pronounce his
words clearly, I told him he would become more self-confident
and begin to feel better about his voice and accent, which were
unique and distinctive.

Poor Grammar

Several clients of mine who are otherwise smart, dynamic, and
extremely talented people demonstrate a fear of falling short of
their professional goals because they are self-conscious over their
habit of using poor grammar.

I use the word *habit* here because these people happen to be
educated and, in some instances, very strong communicators,
except they get lazy with grammar when they speak. We live in a
society that celebrates "relaxed and natural" in all things, including
communicating. In trying to achieve this relaxed and natural style
as speakers, however, we sometimes fail to recognize the distinction between casual and improper. There is such a thing as being
too relaxed, especially in the use of words, and too colloquial.

On the other hand, some people may use improper words in a
public speaking situation because their grammar is weak through
lack of education.

In either case, nothing erodes your credibility faster than
uncertainty over your use of words. Fortunately, poor grammar is
an easy obstacle to overcome. You can take an English course at a
local college, take an online course in grammar, or pick up a self-

help book on improving your grammar (many good ones are available).

Bad Past Experiences (Logistical)

Some people I work with become agitated at the prospect of giving a speech, making a presentation, or being interviewed for a job or for college because they had a bad past experience of a logistical (as opposed to emotional — see chapter 4 for the distinction) nature and are concerned next time will be a case of déjà vu.

For example, maybe the microphone went dead just as you were about to launch into your speech, and the few minutes you spent waiting until — and praying for — the technician to hurry up and kick the microphone back to life again seemed like an eternity.

Or, maybe you tripped on your way to the lectern, and the unnumbered pages of your presentation went flying every which way, forcing you to scramble to retrieve them and, worse, have to make sense out of them again. I even saw a beginner speaker lose his place, not in his presentation but on the stage where he was giving it, and fall into the orchestra pit! That, of course, is an extreme example of a bad past experience, and a rare exception to the typical mishaps that occur, but it's the exception that proves the rule: Stuff happens. And some people can rebound quickly from that stuff and move on, while others panic and become paralyzed. Let's face it, if you've had a bad experience like this once, you can't help but worry at least a little bit that it will happen the next time. There is reality to what you fear; it did happen before. Your fear is justified, but it need not be fueled over and over again until it becomes magnified.

Bad past experiences of this kind drive home the important lesson that there are certain things, like microphones going bad and dropping your prepared text all over the floor, that are unexpected and, therefore, out of your control. But these experiences also drive home another equally, perhaps even more, important message about what *is* in your control. As the saying goes, "Forewarned is forearmed." Past experiences, bad or good, can be great teachers of how to go about achieving a different result next time.

The Good News

The good news about these surface obstacles is that they are just that. They are *surface* issues that are easily addressed—and, in the case of myths, released just by identifying them as such.

So, while you may have been thinking you had an incurable disease, now you have discovered you have only a minor skin irritation, and there is a simple procedure to remove it. You realize you are not suffering from a serious condition, and relief can be immediate, or is not far off.

In the next chapter, however, we are going to dig deeper to reveal the major issues fueling our stage fright, creating obstacles that are more difficult to remove because they are buried beneath the surface.

4

Hidden Obstacles:
Our Six *Dreadly* Fears . . .
and Where They Come From

Let me tell you about Jack. He's a big, tough-looking character who works as a shop foreman at a manufacturing plant in Detroit. He's used to communicating with individuals or small groups when giving orders on the shop floor, a task he handles in a forceful and intense manner, like Robert DeNiro in *Taxi Driver*.

Recently Jack's employers instituted a strategy aimed at stimulating productivity by making employees feel more connected to the overall business. As part of this strategy, Jack and others in positions of authority at the plant were called upon to give a presentation about their respective roles and responsibilities at an upcoming gathering of the company's four hundred-member workforce.

Jack was extremely self-conscious about speaking before such a large group. He was afraid that he'd find himself fumbling for words, turn speechless, and become a pillar of ice. This terrified him because he felt it would make him lose credibility with his workers and appear incompetent to his employers, resulting in a blow to his professional pride and self-esteem that might even cost him his job.

Jack found me via one of my workshops. He was in a total panic. There, in the workshop, I witnessed his fear firsthand as he got up to introduce himself to the others in the group. He stood there, silent. The words just wouldn't come; his humiliation was almost palpable.

With some prodding, I got Jack to loosen up; then I gently took him through the process of uncovering, acknowledging, and clearing away the issue.

I started by asking him to tell me about the best, most positive experience he'd ever had speaking or presenting to a large group.

He said he couldn't remember one.

"Okay," I said. "Then tell me about your worst experience, even if it seems unrelated or even insignificant to you now."

After a fair amount of encouragement from me, and contemplation by Jack, it came to him.

It turns out that when he was a child, his family would gather around the piano in the living room every Sunday and sing songs. Jack looked forward to these sing-alongs each week because he was of an age—around seven or eight—when, unself-consciously, he loved carrying a tune.

During the summer, his family vacationed at a resort that offered a talent show, in which the kids of all the families were encouraged to participate. Jack eagerly signed up to sing the Frank Sinatra classic "I've Got You Under My Skin," a Sunday standard whose music and lyrics he was familiar with.

The night of the talent show, Jack made his way enthusiastically to the stage. As the accompanist launched into the oldie-but-goodie on the piano, Jack looked out at the audience, which included his father, mother, and siblings; he opened his mouth to sing, then . . . hesitated.

He didn't recognize the music being played.

Was it the intro?

The refrain?

He froze.

"What happened next?" I asked. "What did you do?"

Though clearly uncomfortable with the memory he was recalling, Jack continued to dredge.

"I . . . didn't know what to do," he said. "So . . . I just started to leave the stage."

But before he could get off, his father came out of the audience, went up onto the stage, grabbed him by the shoulders, and shook him, shouting (in front of everyone): "You're going to stay here and finish that song!"

I find this story heartbreaking but also not uncommon.

Many people experience tremendous anxiety associated with communicating in front of groups or with other people. In cases where the anxiety isn't as deeply rooted as Jack's, it may simply have a restricting effect. But in other cases, like Jack's, it can be totally debilitating because it's been compensated for and nursed a long time—perhaps since childhood, adolescence, or early in our careers.

Until our workshop, Jack had never really thought about, much less consciously grasped, the significance of that incident in his youth. To him, it was an unpleasant but long-ago memory, nothing more. And yet in the context of his ability to communicate confidently and comfortably before a large group, it had powerful and unintended consequences on his daily life.

The surface obstacles I described in the previous chapter impede or erode our confidence as speakers because of the myths we harbor about what it takes to be a first-rate communicator or because of skills we may lack. Personal experiences from our past, often our childhoods, that hamper us—what I call hidden obstacles—operate on a deeper, more insidious level.

If we can identify the hidden obstacle that fuels our individual stage fright and unlock the mystery of it, it's possible to be free of it once and for all or, at the very least, get it under control.

This may sound a bit oversimplified, but I can assure you that after years of helping hundreds upon hundreds of clients explore the roots of their performance anxiety (and just as many years delving into the roots of my own), I know that if you are determined to be free of your fear of facing an audience, the answer really is that simple.

Our Six *Dreadly* Fears . . .

Listening for so long to hundreds of clients talk about their past experiences with stage fright, I've been able to catalog and describe the following most common fears we have about public speaking that become hidden obstacles. These hidden obstacles indicate that there is more to performance anxiety than just buying into a myth about public speaking or being impeded by a skill-related roadblock.

1. Fear of Criticism or Being Judged (Negatively)

This fear can be excruciating. With some people, it causes them not to try at all, because they feel that whatever they do won't be good enough. In others, this fear makes them overcompensate by preparing so much that they leave no room for spontaneity.

Kevin, for example, was a bright high school senior who scored a perfect 1600 on his SATs. He was a virtual shoo-in for acceptance at any college of his choosing and was preparing for his first college interview when his mother and father came to me for help.

I asked them what the problem was, and they told me that Kevin was very shy in situations where he had to get up in front of people. He was having a lot of difficulty preparing for the interview, they said.

In our discussions, Kevin revealed that his greatest challenge in high school was speaking up in class. He just couldn't bring himself to do it, even though he had the smarts and was academically sophisticated enough not to have to worry about embarrassing himself.

So, what was he afraid of?

From working with others like Kevin (most of them adults) and having survived adolescence myself, I knew that his discomfort at being thrust center stage probably stemmed from a fear of criticism.

In an effort to root out why he felt this way, I asked him about his interests and what he wanted to study in college. They were the same, he said; he had always loved animals and wanted to be a researcher in animal diseases or a veterinarian. I already knew this because I'd posed the same question to Kevin's parents. I had asked them what it was about studying animals that interested their son.

"I really don't know," his father answered. "Kevin's never shown any interest in sports like I did growing up. Just studying animals."

Kevin's father worriedly assumed, as many parents do in similar situations, that his child was "different" from other kids.

Kevin had picked up on this message. His shyness and lack of confidence stemmed, in large part, from his fear of being characterized as different by his peers. It was a significant piece of the puzzle.

I explained to Kevin how my work has shown me that we are all "different." The differences are also what make us unique. His affinity for animals and desire to help them was a passion; he should feel good about that—many people lack passion of any kind. I told him that even if it was a different course than his parents might have chosen (as is the case with many of us), he should be confident about pursuing it precisely because he was so passionate about it. If he focused on the passion itself rather than on how different he thought it made him seem, and communicated authentically from that position, his parents—whom I knew to be wonderful people who truly loved their son—would support him emotionally and in his career goals 100 percent, and he would be able to speak from the heart with enthusiasm and self-confidence to anyone.

Kevin went for the interview—in fact he had several at a number of schools where he'd applied—and was accepted at the one he'd had his eye on all along because of its distinguished veterinary program.

It took just two sessions of working with Kevin to uncover his hidden dissuader and to help him develop the physical skills he needed to project his natural, authentic self with ease. So, even though mining for that hidden dissuader can sometimes be difficult, it doesn't take years to root out and vanquish. Nothing, not even fear of criticism, is irreversible. And it's never too late to start.

2. Fear of Forgetting

There are several reasons for this fear. Some are easy to fix, while others are more complex, requiring closer inspection in order to be resolved.

For example, when you get overly concerned about going blank in the middle of a presentation or job interview, your focus becomes misplaced, and you increase the odds of doing exactly what you fear. Your focus should be on preparation and rehearsal instead; it's having too little of either or both that typically causes those "senior moments" in the spotlight in the first place.

That's the easiest type of fear of forgetting to address. But there could be other sources of such a fear, as in the case of Jane.

Jane was in charge of a local credit union where she was required to conduct large staff meetings on a regular basis. She lived in constant panic that she would lose her place going over the itinerary, draw a total blank in the middle of the meeting, and come off looking unprofessional, perhaps even ridiculous. She prepared and rehearsed for these meetings as I directed her, working very hard to fight back her fear. And yet the fear persisted.

I asked her if there was any time in her experience—childhood, adolescence, adulthood—that she could recall actually having drawn a blank in front of a group.

She pondered my question for a second, and said, "No, I don't remember anything like that."

"Okay," I said, "keep thinking about it, and if something comes to mind, let me know at our next session."

When she arrived for the next session, she told me she'd done what I'd asked her and had remembered something, though it wasn't at all related to business.

She described being in a high school play and rehearsing her part for a month after school until she had all her lines down pat. The night of the performance, she stepped out onstage, opened her mouth to speak, and all those lines she knew so well just wouldn't come out.

"I went totally blank," she said.

"So, what did you do?" I asked.

"I just stood there," she said. "I felt so foolish. Someone else in the cast had to jump in with some lines to cover the silence."

I asked her how she felt as she was relating this story, and she answered, "Uncomfortable." That incident, which she thought she'd put out of her mind as just one of those things that happen to everybody growing up, still made her squirm when she conjured it up, she said, seeing the connection between it and her present anxiety for the first time. In fact, this high school incident was not just one of those things; it was quite relevant to her present fear of forgetting at a staff meeting, and as such it deserved to be addressed.

Were the emotional repercussions of that childhood incident the only source of Jane's fear of forgetting whenever she had to conduct a staff meeting? Probably not. Nevertheless, there was a clear and direct correlation between it and her current difficulties.

In exploring the roots of your own fears (if I've made this sound too scary, let me say now that the expedition can also be fun), keep in mind that you are looking for issues dealing with "performance" only. If you have emotional problems that go beyond the scope of this book, problems that affect you on a much broader level, a deeper examination from a professional psychologist or psychiatrist who is equipped to deal with these more complex issues may be required.

3.   Fear of Embarrassment or Humiliation

The last thing any of us wants to do is to put ourselves in a position where we might embarrass ourselves publicly. It's pretty high on just about everyone's list of things to avoid. The dread of such a situation can be crippling.

Seasoned speakers and presenters live with this fear like most of us, but they keep it at bay by preparing well ahead of time and building in a contingency plan for the inevitable dangers that lurk beyond the edge of the lectern, the stage, or the conference table. This enables them to approach their public speaking task with confidence, knowing that whatever happens—and "stuff" always will—they will likely be able to handle it with ease and grace. They recognize the fact that they are human and thus vulnerable to making mistakes. Knowing that sooner or later Murphy's Law will come into play, they live by my mantra: "It's not the mistake, it's how you recover!"

This is an important principle, one that I learned early on in my career as a performer and have carried with me ever since. Inexperienced speakers, presenters, and interviewees, however, often can't get beyond their fear of being embarrassed. They suffer from severely debilitating symptoms of anticipation waiting for the hour when they must thrust themselves into the limelight, and they walk around with a sense of dread from the firm conviction that they will never survive the ordeal. Or, they'll opt out of putting themselves through the ordeal by avoiding the situation altogether, often to the detriment of their careers.

For example, Elizabeth, a young woman whose fear of getting up in front of people and embarrassing herself was almost palpable, shared this story in one of my workshops. She told us about a time in high school, which was not all that long ago for her, when she and her classmates had to stand up and recite a poem they were reading in class.

"I kept mispronouncing a particular word," she said, "so the teacher made me go to the front of the class and hop on one foot, saying the word over and over until I got it right." I couldn't believe what I was hearing. I thought this type of "teaching" went out with the Dark Ages, but apparently it's still with us.

Stories like Elizabeth's very often are behind the fear of embarrassment we may feel when we are called upon to speak in public or communicate in any formal setting. These experiences are tremendous blows to our self-esteem that may leave considerable personal devastation in their wake.

The bad news is that if you don't work through the fear by pinpointing the source and clearing it away, it will very likely continue to get the better of you. And you will be severely limiting yourself personally and professionally by using only a fraction of your most important capability: the power to speak for yourself.

The good news, though, is that this doesn't have to happen. Like Elizabeth in our workshop, you too can succeed in turning your fear of embarrassment into a thing of the past.

4. Fear of Failure (or Success)

These fears are really two sides of the same coin.

Imagine, if you will, a young man about to graduate from high school, where he demonstrated the prowess of a pro baseball player on the school team. Some major-league scouts have seen him play, and the young man is thunderstruck to be invited to try out for a pro team. The young man's father has always been proud of his son's athletic accomplishments in school, but the young man never tells his father about the tryout invitation. The thought of disappointing his father by failing to make the team, or, even worse, succeeding in making the team but then failing to make the grade later on creates too much pressure for the young man.

The day of the tryout finally arrives.

The young man's plan is to leave the house that morning when he usually does, just as if he's following his normal daily routine, then to catch a bus to and from the tryout without anyone but him being the wiser. But then, at the last moment, just as he's about to climb onto that bus . . .

He can't bring himself to do it.

He steps back.

The door shuts. And the bus pulls away.

The risk of failing, or succeeding now only to possibly fail later, has proven too much for him, the fear too great. So, he never tries out, and never knows whether he would have made the team and had a major-league career or not. No risk, no failure. Easy. But, of course, not so easy—because these questions will haunt him for the rest of his life.

The young man had prepared himself for the tryout by developing the skills he needed to land an invitation, but he hadn't completed his preparation because he never addressed the hidden dissuader that would ultimately prevent him from following through and getting on that bus. If this type of behavior sets in and becomes habitual, he won't need any obstacles to make him keep scoring a near miss; he'll continually be short-circuiting his own opportunities.

5.   Fear of the Unknown

Remember the excitement we felt as children when we were going on a camping trip or a family vacation? We couldn't wait to get there. We were ready to conquer the world, ready for whatever adventure awaited us, not knowing—and totally unconcerned about not knowing—what lay ahead.

Then an unfortunate thing happened.

We grew up and became adults.

We started to overplan, overprepare, and overconcern our-selves with minutiae that, in many cases, were beyond our capac-ity to master. In short, we spoiled our fun.

Sure you have to make travel plans, book hotel rooms, perhaps even make arrangements for certain activities before going on a trip. But it's also important to leave room for those deliciously unexpected moments of spontaneity that many times turn out to be the best part of any trip.

What does this have to do with speaking without fear?

You're planning to give a speech or make a presentation to a group of twenty or, maybe, hundreds. As the event draws near, you become intrinsically aware that all of your preplanning (in fact, all the preplanning in the world) won't see you through the unexpected things that can, and likely will, occur—for example, that management crisis that comes crashing down on you the morning of the event, throwing a monkey wrench into your whole day and leaving you wrung out and overstressed by the time you have to step to the podium and . . . be charming to all those expec-tant faces.

Aware that a scenario like that could occur no matter how much preplanning you do, you begin to panic—because you sud-denly realize that the worst thing you can imagine happening, just did. *You lost control.*

In public speaking situations, fear of the unknown translates to fear of losing control. In order to feel safe, we feel we must control every variable—human, environmental, technical. And yet, as in life, this just isn't realistic. Controlling everything that's around that corner simply isn't possible. Having said that, however, I ask you to listen carefully: controlling your fear of losing control *is* possible.

6. Fear of Bad Past Experiences (Emotional)

If you flopped as a public speaker in the past, or botched a previous job interview and think you'll do so again, chances are you probably will. The reason why is that thought typically precedes action. Negative thoughts triggered by negative emotions will likely yield negative outcomes.

In other words, the theory is that our bodies recognize negative thoughts and respond accordingly. I happen to believe this theory and am by no means alone in doing so. Volumes have been written about it, and we've all seen it demonstrated.

For example, we've seen a skier or a gymnast take a terrible spill, then get up and go on—maybe a little shakily at first but able to get right back on track. We've also seen others take similar, even lesser, spills, and be unable to regain their confidence and composure. What spells the difference? Part of it is skill and experience, of course, but the key element is how we *think*.

I once attended a seminar on this topic at the Fashion Institute of Technology in New York City. All of us in the audience were asked to partner up. The seminar leader then selected one member of each team to be the subject. That person was instructed to hold his or her arm out straight, shoulder height, parallel to the floor, while letting the other arm fall limply to the side in a relaxed position. The subject was then told to think of a pleasant experience or person that made him or her happy, and to hold that thought. "Nod when you're ready," the leader said.

The other partner was then told to press down as hard as possible on the extended arm while the subject concentrated on the happy thought, offering as much resistance as possible. Whether the subject was a woman and the partner a much stronger man had no impact on the result, which was the same for 80 percent of the teams. The partner was unable to move the subject's outstretched arm. Resistance was too strong. The arm refused to budge.

The seminar leader then reversed the instruction. This time the subject was asked to think of a situation or person that made him or her unhappy, and to hold that thought while the partner once more pushed down on the subject's arm. The result was the same—except that in this go-around 80 percent of the arms went down, offering little or no resistance no matter how hard the subject tried.

A negative mind-set will most likely yield a negative result. This is an important rule not only when it comes to public speaking but in all aspects of life. If you think you will fail, you probably will. But if you are bound and determined not to fail, you will likely take steps to ensure that you won't. The truth is, if you've had an emotionally traumatic experience as a public speaker in the past—for example, freezing up like Jack in the story at the beginning of this chapter—you have, like Jack as well, a *choice* as to how you handle the future.

. . . and Where They Come From

How did we come to be held in the grip of these Dreadly Fears? We certainly didn't wake up one morning and say, "Gee, I don't want to go to school today because I have a fear of failure." Or, "I'm purposely going to lose that debate this afternoon because I have a fear of success."

These common hidden obstacles stem from powerful negative messages we've received at some point in our lives that we have internalized and nurtured over the years, bestowing upon them a hold over us in the form of inhibitions that, in most cases, they were never intended to have and do not warrant.

These powerful negative messages are transmitted to us by one (or, perhaps, *all*) of the following sources:

- level 1 transmitters: our parents
- level 2 transmitters: siblings
- level 3 transmitters: peers and outside-the-home authority figures (i.e., teachers, ministers, et al.)

Not a Blame Game

Let me state something very clearly here so that there is no confusion. If a negative observation or cutting remark made to us in our formative years by someone important in our life is still playing havoc with our ability to speak fearlessly, we must recognize that the power this observation or remark continues to have on us is something *we have allowed*.

As adults, we are responsible for charting our own course in life. Whether we elect to remain stuck in the past or to move forward and create a new possibility for ourselves is a decision that is entirely up to us.

Level 1 Transmitters—Our Parents

A friend of mine teaches ballet to inexperienced as well as trained dancers. Recently, she offered this observation about how she gives feedback to her students. "Basically, there are three types of feedback," she says. "Constructive, destructive, and too early. Telling someone they'll be a great dancer when they have little or no grace and rhythm is not only unrealistic but an injustice. But telling them they have no grace and rhythm and are defective because of this is damaging to their self-image."

As a teacher, she is acutely aware of the power of her remarks. If one of her beginner students demonstrates no signs of ever becoming a great ballerina, she still encourages that student to keep trying, without fear of embarrassment, to achieve her personal best because by honing whatever degree of talent she does possess, the student will develop a self-discipline that will serve her well in the future going after more realistic pursuits.

"If I can keep them from giving up too soon, who knows how far they'll get?" my friend says. Her whole philosophy is to let her students reach the decision themselves about whether or not they have the right stuff to pursue a professional career in ballet. "At least their self-image stays intact, and more than anything else—except, perhaps for good health—that arms them to handle almost anything that will come their way in life," she says. Unfortunately, many of the people in our lives who influence our self-esteem don't possess my teacher friend's professional awareness of the power of their words.

While the remarks of our siblings, peers, teachers, and so on may have a potent impact on what we come to accept, even believe, as truths, the most powerful human transmitters of the messages that shape our attitudes, our perceptions of the world, and how we feel about ourselves are our parents (or other primary caregivers).

Their influence starts, literally, from the day we're born, because their words rule during the key years of our development. That's why the performance-anxiety issues that their words may intentionally or unintentionally stir in us have such strong roots and are among the toughest to dig out and cast off.

Doug switched careers in his midforties to take an important management position in a major corporation. He came to the job from a creative background, where his skill working with all kinds of people to push through all kinds of projects attracted the eye of his current employer. In his new position, he is responsible not only for overseeing a large department but giving quarterly pep talks to the large group of company analysts he oversees.

The first thing I noticed about Doug when he came to me for help polishing his delivery is how funny, engaging, extremely articulate, energetic, and self-confident he is in expressing his ideas. As he spoke, I found that he really made me listen. But then, as I watched him give one of his quarterly pep talks to his employees, I witnessed another Doug emerge: the public Doug, who was inhibited and self-conscious. He spoke haltingly and barely above a whisper, so that it was all but impossible to hear him.

We made some adjustments to his technique, such as making more eye contact and projecting his voice, which should have resulted in a more dynamic performance. But he still remained low-key and unexpressive, unable to employ these techniques. Our work wasn't finished.

As Doug and I explored the problem, he revealed that he found it extremely difficult to be physically expressive in front of groups. When I asked him why, he answered at first that he didn't know why. But eventually it came out that Doug's parents were highly respected members of the community, and as such, they told him all the while he was growing up that it was inappropriate to call attention to yourself in public. Doing so, they said, branded you as a show-off.

I explained that communicating to an audience required a certain amount of showing off, in the sense of having to summon and exhibit more physical energy than you normally would one-on-one, in order to get your point across.

"It's the difference between playing only to the front row of a theater because those are the only people you want to reach, and playing to the front *and* back rows of the theater if your goal is to reach the entire audience," I said. The family dictum about what constituted showing off was undermining his ability to perform a key part of his job successfully. I told him that I was not suggesting he transform himself, just that he needed to inject a lot more bounce to the ounce into his "performance" so as not to be perceived by his audience as irresolute, self-conscious, and unsure. Prior to our discussion, he had absolutely no idea that he came off so poorly in such situations. It was decidedly not the image that he sought to project — that of the strong, self-assured leader who boosted the confidence of his troops.

The implications of his parents' words went even deeper, though. Their message, delivered to Doug the boy, had generated a power struggle that was still going on all these years later within Doug the now-middle-aged man. It was a struggle over just how visible — i.e., successful — Doug could allow himself to become in life, yet not be labeled a show-off. Though it was certainly not transmitted to him with the intent of doing Doug any emotional harm, his parents' message about showing off had done precisely that. Their words had helped to manufacture in their son an attitude or belief that was not serving him well in his adult pursuits.

Once this was out on the table, everything fell quickly into place for Doug. He did not wallow in self-pity by thinking of himself as a victim, nor did he feel an angry need to confront and chastise his parents for the effect of their words (which had been unintended) in order to vanquish his inhibition. Recognizing its existence and identifying its source were sufficient in releasing it.

Subsequently, he learned from me how to use his body language and his voice to animate and project his ideas to an audience so that his employees would actively listen and stay involved as he spoke. He is able to speak openly and comfortably in many different kinds of public situations now. He even admits to some real "showing off" now and then, "but only just a little bit."

The intent behind other parental messages that influence us may not be quite so benign, however. Nor are the repercussions. One woman I worked with was already a dynamite speaker, so strutting her stuff wasn't the problem. She had it all: professional appearance, great smile, solid technique. However, before every speech, she threw herself into excruciating panic. I asked what she was so afraid might happen, and she said she was afraid she wouldn't live up to the audience's expectations of her, and people would conclude that she wasn't really what she projected herself to be.

Where did this fear come from? I wondered. As we explored it further, it emerged that she had been raised by very demanding parents. If she brought home a report card with anything less than straight A's, she would be scolded severely for not living up to her potential and be sternly warned that her future was at stake.

"I remember getting a report card once with an A-plus, three A's, and two B's on it," she said. "My folks hit the roof! 'How could you do this to *us*?' they shouted. 'How can you give us B's when we are working so hard to give you everything you need to get A's? At this rate, you'll *never* amount to anything!'"

Only after sharing this story did she fully begin to understand what was truly at the bottom of the panic she felt prior to stepping before the podium. She'd tossed off that report card incident from her childhood, and other incidents like it, as "just the way things were." Now, she agreed, it was important to take another look at those incidents, and their repercussions, from her present perspective as a mature adult and settle the underlying issues.

This is the point of mining our personal stories and sharing what they may reveal to us. We seek to identify those level 1 messages that have become our thorniest—and stickiest—hidden obstacles. Such messages from our parents and other primary caregivers act like red lights, signaling us to STOP! We must change that signal to a green light in order to become powerful, persuasive communicators.

Common Level 1 Transmissions

These are some typical parental messages my clients have identified as personal roadblocks to becoming confident, comfortable public speakers and communicators. Use this list as a memory jogger, or as a starting point, to find your own hidden dissuader, if one exists. It will help you with the clearing-out process later on in chapter 5.

"Children should be seen and not heard."
"You'll never amount to anything."
"Don't be a show-off."
"You'd have to be a lot smarter for people to want to hear what you have to say."
"Your sister is the pretty, talented one."
"Your brother is a people person, not you."

Level 2 Transmitters—Siblings

Though not as influential as those of our parents, negative messages from our siblings have tremendous power in shaping how we see ourselves. Again, as with a level 1 transmission, the extent of the damage our siblings' comments may cause is determined by the potency of the comment and the point we were at in our lives when the comment was made.

Some siblings are tremendously supportive of one another, while other siblings are so competitive that, like Cain and Abel, only one can survive!

Does this story ring familiar? One of my clients told me that when she was a little girl she was asked to sing in a local charity talent show because she had such a lovely voice. After the show, her sister, who was about a year or two younger, commented that she had sung off key during the show, and then delivered the coup de grâce. "You just can't carry a tune!" the sister told her.

To this day, my client, who always did and still does possess a lovely voice, cannot bring herself to sing in public. In fact, the power of her sibling's negative comment, regardless of its having been motivated by obvious jealousy rather than fact, has continued to nibble at my client's self-confidence in other areas of public performing, such as giving presentations to coworkers and clients.

This is not uncommon. Whether a message transmitted by a sibling when we're growing up is meant to wound us just briefly out of jealousy or is a direct shot fired across our bow with the intention of sinking us, its negative effect can be lasting, and one of the areas where that negative effect will surface as an inhibitor is almost any forum where we must take the stage. We hang on to cutting remarks from our brothers and sisters, especially those that cut the deepest, as if they were spoken yesterday, allowing them to grow into shields we use to hold us back. As a result, we limit the range of our emotional resources, using only a small capacity of what's available to us.

Level 3 Transmitters—
Peers and Authority Figures Outside the Home

Peers

If you watch children at play, you will notice an interesting difference between the genders. Boys sling barbs at each other and play one-upmanship, then walk away seemingly comfortable and totally unfazed by the competition, no matter how intense it was.

For example, a typical exchange between boys greeting each other might go something like this:

"Hey, how ya doin'? That's one ugly shirt you got on, dude."

Common Level 2 Transmissions

These are some typical negative messages from siblings as reported by people in my workshops. Identify your hidden dissuader from this list, or, if it's not on the list, add it. If you've got a hidden dissuader, this exercise will help with the clearing-out process in chapter 5.

"My sister told me that when I get up to speak, I look and sound just like our mother. I don't like our mother and don't want to be like her!"

"Sis, you can't tell a joke or a story to save your neck."

"Your brother and I are smart. How come you're not?"

"My sister says my voice grates."

"You're fat and nobody likes you."

"Let me do the talking. Everything you say comes out wrong."

"So's your face, man."

Here's the rule among boys in such situations: At all costs thou shalt not demonstrate any hurt.

Now imagine a young girl walking up to another and saying, "Hi! Wow, that's an ugly dress you're wearing, and where did you get those awful shoes?"

The response in this case would probably be a whole lot different, as the recipient of the remark moved from a soft whimper to a full-blown wail and ran home to hide out in her room for days. Different approaches for different genders.

I don't need to reiterate here what experts in the field of child psychology have said and written on the subject of peer pressure in our development. We've all been there. If you ever missed the answer to a question on an oral exam in front of the whole class and felt the scorn (real or imagined) of your classmates, then you understand the influence peers can have. Years later, as your boss calls on you in a staff meeting for an update on the department's sales figures, you may suddenly feel yourself breaking into a sweat and think to yourself, without even knowing why, "Oh, my god! What if I put my foot in my mouth?" That's just how powerful the good or bad messages we get from our peers can be in our lives. Painful peer exchanges do, in fact, linger. But they don't have to. They can and should be brought to the surface so they can be replaced by positive feelings that serve more positive needs.

Remember how important it was in grade school, high school, and even college to be "cool"? The word *cool*, which is still in use, translates to what is currently fashionable and what is not. God forbid you ever cross the line, or you'll be banished to the land of the uncool.

Every generation defines its standards of what is cool and what is not, and it's hard to challenge those standards. Courage is being who you are and risking negative judgment. That's legitimate cool. I wonder if Eleanor Roosevelt, Stephen Covey, or Bill Gates were considered uncool by their peers while growing up? If so, they got the last laugh, didn't they?

One of my clients is gay. All the while growing up, he felt deeply uncomfortable about his emerging sexuality. At play or in class, whenever he showed enthusiasm or excitement, his physical gestures tended toward the "effeminate," prompting his peers to make fun of him. Today, though, he is well and comfortably out of the closet. But whenever he has to give a presentation, he's emotionally transported back to his school days, and he tries to suppress any emerging signs of "effeminacy" in his performance. He overcompensates with a delivery style that is static, humorless, and without energy. His style borders on being a caricature of the stereotypical "man in the gray flannel suit," which isn't him at all.

As we talked and I began to realize what was actually going on, I addressed the issue gingerly, pointing out that when he didn't bring more of who he really was to his presentation, his audience of customers and clients sensed on an instinctive level that something was wrong. This translated to a lack of credibility on his part, perhaps even a lack of honesty.

Authority Figures Outside the Home

The second most influential source of damaging level 3 transmissions are the unsolicited, unwanted, and sometimes downright thoughtless remarks of a teacher, a guidance counselor, a coach, a minister, or some other figure in a position of authority and respect with whom we come in contact during our formative years.

I cannot number how many stories I've heard in my workshops about incidents from clients' childhoods or adolescence in which they bore the brunt of a stinging criticism or negative remark from an adult who was not their parent but whom they'd been taught to hold in high esteem. And because they were kids, they believed what the adult said must be true and carried that "truth" with them for a long, sometimes *very* long, time!

For example, Steven was a midlevel executive eager to move up the ladder of the fast-paced PR firm where he was currently marketing manager. He was a charming, sweet, soft-spoken guy—a real pussycat. Which was precisely the trouble. His manner was so self-effacing that he made you want to hug him rather than buy what he had to sell—not exactly a big plus for an ambitious marketing and sales type.

I suggested to Steven that he add some juice to the way he was presenting himself by, first, pumping up the volume. He did. And then an odd thing happened. He actually grew quieter and quieter until he became so indistinct that none of us in the workshop could hear him.

"Excuse me, Steven," I interrupted. "Perhaps you misunderstood me. Could you speak louder? We're having trouble hearing you."

"I have trouble speaking loud," he said. "I feel like I'm over-powering people, and they don't like that."

I agreed with him that overpowering one's listeners is a no-no, but he had many more decibels to go before that would happen.

He asked if he could say something more about this issue, and I encouraged him to go ahead. He told of an incident when he was in the sixth grade. He'd just moved to the area, and this was his first year in the new school. Student elections were coming up, and he decided to take part. He ran for class president, and being a nat-ural charmer who made friends easily, he won a lot of supporters.

As the election drew near, it came down to a tight two-person race between him and another student who had lived in the school district for years. A final debate was held to determine the win-ning candidate. Steven was about to take his place at the podium to deliver the campaign speech he hoped would put him over the top when the teacher who was supervising the election (and who would decide its outcome) came up to him and remarked how unfair it would be for Steven to become sixth-grade class presi-dent rather than the other boy just because Steven was more pop-ular and a newcomer.

"I died," Steven told us. "After the teacher said that to me, I went to give my speech and just froze. Nothing came out. The class applauded anyway. But the election was over."

Basically, this authority figure had reprimanded young Steven for being outgoing and personable. The boy took this negative message to heart because, after all, it came from a teacher so it must be true; now, even as an adult, when addressing a group of people, even a small number like our workshop, he would sup-press his natural energy, charisma, and persuasive power so as not to be misconstrued as trying to "get it over on anyone."

You may now have an idea of what is at play in your particular situation, preventing you from ever feeling competent in a speak-ing setting. Each situation and person are different, and what you must remember is that only you have the key to unlock this door.

Common Level 3 Transmissions

These are some typical negative messages from peers and authority figures such as teachers and clergy, which people in my workshops have come up with. Identify your hidden dissuader from this list, or, if it's not on the list, add it. If you've got a hidden dissuader, this exercise will help with the clearing process in chapter 5.

"This is a public *speaking* class; keep your hands still and to the side!"

"That was a stupid answer. Take your seat."

"You might as well give up now. Children from your background never make it."

"If you're in the school play you will ruin the production."

"Women must be reserved and hide signs of intelligence."

"There will be no displays of emotion on this team."

"Your recital wasn't perfect. You missed a note."

In the next chapter you are going to learn how to identify your specific problem and go on to the issue of clearing out the emotional residue from unwanted messages that are impeding your progress.

5

Clearing Your Instrument and Getting Beyond What's Holding You Back

A Matter of Authenticity

As a young and aspiring actress it was exciting for me to be able to express myself through the voices of so many different characters. But as I got older it became more important for me to find my own voice. I think this is what we all strive for as public speakers: to communicate naturally and easily to others that extra ingredient that is uniquely and strongly us—whether it's our humor, our passion, or both.

I may encounter an unpolished speaker who holds me in his or her thrall, while the words of a polished professional may strike me as sounding ho-hum. Very often, the difference can be summed up in one word: authenticity.

Authenticity is what we respond to most strongly as listeners. Therefore, what I encourage my clients to work toward as speakers and communicators is to achieve a style of communicating that is a reflection of who they truly are, not a false notion or imitation of something or someone else they think they should be.

The dictionary definition of *authentic* is *genuine*. When we sense from a speaker's words that he or she is genuine, we find that person credible and, therefore, characterize him or her as trustworthy and possessing integrity.

Being authentic means acknowledging that we share a commonality of human experience and have the skill to shape our messages in ways that build understanding. It requires us to know a lot about ourselves and what makes us tick. It is personal—it is about us as individuals and what is inside of us.

Feeling good about who you are is critical to achieving an authentic communication style, one that you will hone for the rest of your life as your attitudes change and who you are is reshaped by new experiences. The best of the best strive to find new ways to bring more of their authentic selves to their communications.

Creating such a possibility for yourself can be an extremely rewarding process. But the key word here is *process*. Only when your instrument is clear can your authentic voice resonate loud and strong.

Let's begin by discovering and clearing out the hidden obstacle that is either impeding you or holding you back completely from making that speech, giving that presentation, or going for that interview.

There are four exercises involved in the clearing process:

Exercise #1: *Discover and Acknowledge*
Exercise #2: *Release*
Exercise #3: *Reframe*
Exercise #4: *Visualize and Make Real*

If you have a public speaking engagement, a presentation, a job or college interview in the offing, these exercises, in combination with the set of practical skills you will learn in part 2, will prepare you to meet these challenges and seize the opportunities they present in a way you've never experienced before.

As far in advance of your next speech, presentation, or interview as time will allow, complete each exercise in sequence before moving on to the next—*and resist the temptation to jump ahead.*

How often should you repeat this process?

That depends.

My recommendation for Avoiders and Anticipators is that they work through all four exercises each time a public performance beckons, until the day arrives (and it will come sooner than they can now imagine) when they will hear themselves respond to the idea of public speaking with an enthusiastic "Yes!"

Adrenalizers and Improvisers on the other hand may not need to go through all four more than once. My recommendation is that several days before an upcoming performance situation, they go through exercises 3 and 4 (until no longer needed) as a way of harnessing their energy and/or focusing their priority on the tasks that need to be completed.

Exercise #1: Discover and Acknowledge

On a blank piece of paper, draw a line down the center of the page. At the top of the left column, print the following:

"The **worst** that could happen . . ."

Now, think fast and list the negative outcome(s) you most often fear will happen when you have to get up and speak in front of people, make a presentation to a group, or be interviewed for a job or a promotion (see figure 1). For example, some of you might respond: "*I'm afraid I'll . . .*"

- "lose my place."
- "go blank."
- "be criticized."
- "look foolish."
- "forget what I'm saying and grope for words."
- "be laughed at."

Be spontaneous and honest with yourself. Don't question or edit your responses. There is no right or wrong here. Jot down the fears that spring quickest to your mind. It doesn't matter whether you come up with a list of three or thirty.

Figure 1

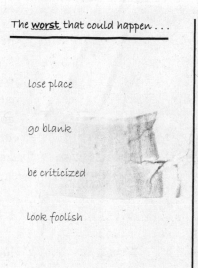

The **worst** that could happen . . .

lose place

go blank

be criticized

look foolish

Once you've got your list of "worsts," look them over and, below them, in the same column, write down how each one resonates with you as you consider it (see figure 2) — in other words, how do you feel about it? If you notice you start to experience a strong emotional or even physical response, you are on the right track. For example, being afraid of criticism may make you feel embarrassed or humiliated, whereas the prospect of going blank may make you feel a surge of anger or tightness in your chest.

On the other hand, as you consider your feelings about each "worst" on your list, it's quite possible that you might feel just mildly uncomfortable at the thought of it. That's okay too. Again, there is no right or wrong here.

Figure 2

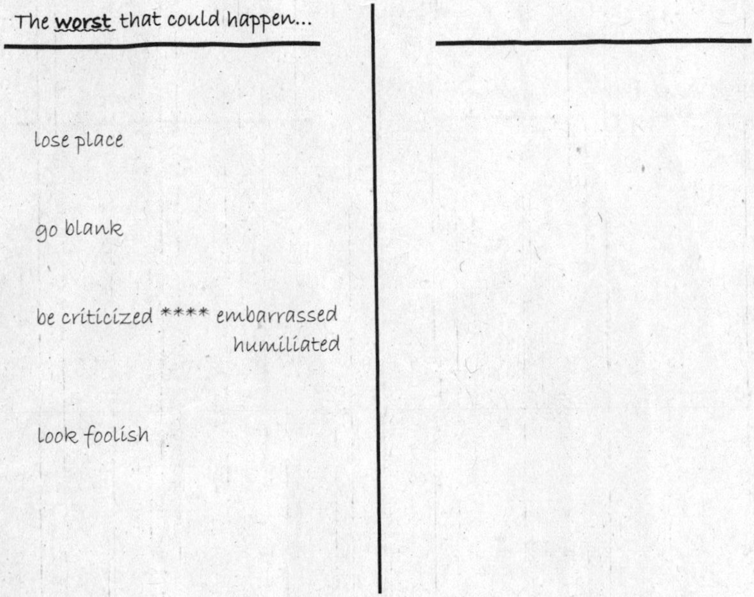

The **worst** that could happen...

_____

lose place

go blank

be criticized **** embarrassed
                    humiliated

look foolish

After you have gone through this part of the exercise, you will now have an idea, or at least an instinct, about which "worst" gives you the strongest negative feeling (or you may find they all have equal weight). Let's say your feeling of being embarrassed at being criticized really hits you where it hurts. Now, think back through your life experiences and try to recall a time when you were in a performance situation where you felt embarrassed at being criticized, with the same degree of emotional intensity you're feeling now at the prospect of being similarly embarrassed. By "performance situation" I mean any incident similar to speaking before a group or making a presentation to an audience, no matter how tenuous or even remote the similarity might strike you.

Be honest with yourself. As you're doing this in the privacy of your own home, you can afford to be—and the more honest you are, the more rewarding the results of this exercise will be for you.

As you recall the incident (or incidents) in your past, take note of what you're feeling emotionally at the recollection, as well as any physical sensation(s), if any, that may accompany, and therefore add to, your discomfort. For example, one of my clients experienced a literal pain in her eye as she recalled and reexperienced some long-ago feeling of humiliation. Another felt a tightness in his chest.

What this compels you to do is discover the underlying issue (the level 1, 2, or 3 transmission) behind your fear, and to acknowledge the negative emotion connected with that issue that you have internalized and nurtured. You must discover and acknowledge that issue before you can move on to clearing away the negative emotion connected with it.

Exercise #2: Release

Before getting into this exercise, I want to reemphasize why you are doing it. If you find yourself in a truly heightened state of anxiety at the thought of speaking in public or giving a presentation, it is necessary to approach the problem from an emotional, physical, and spiritual perspective, not just a practical one, in order to achieve a total and sustained solution.

Your ability to effect change in yourself and leave a positive impression on any size audience requires you to be fully present, which is to say in the here and now. If you are consciously or subconsciously holding on to something in the past, you aren't fully present. And it is being fully present that gives you the spontaneity, the freedom, and the reaction time to be naturally responsive to your audience.

So, how do we become fully present?

Once you have isolated the past experience(s) and identified the intense emotion triggering the stress reaction creating your anxiety, you will want to bring that emotion to the surface in such a way that you can diminish its leverage until its powerful hold on you no longer exists. A simple but effective tool for doing this, which I adapted from a method used by a friend of mine who is a grief recovery specialist, is called journaling.

As you recall that incident or experience in your past that continues to produce a stress reaction when you think about it, write a description in a memo pad, personal diary, or other type of journal. There is no minimum or maximum page limit here. Just keep writing until you feel you've said it all. Be specific. Tell in detail what happened, who was there, what they said or did, how you felt at the time, and, most important, how you are feeling now in terms of anxiety as you recall that experience. Begin the process by assessing the intensity of your level of anxiety. Give your anxiety level a number on a 1-to-10 scale, with "1" being "low anxiety" and "10" being "high anxiety."

As you go about your business over the next several months, weeks, days, or even hours leading up to your presentation or interview, each time a negative thought about what you're facing creeps into your mind and starts to seize hold of your emotions, go back to your journal and write again. Keep a record of the intensity of your anxiety on the same 1-to-10 scale. Again, be honest with yourself. For example, let's say when you start this exercise you honestly feel you are a "10" on the Anxiety Meter. But after noting your anxiety level once or twice a day or however often you ponder your upcoming performance, you decide that in your honest judgment your anxiety level has suddenly dropped to, say, a "7." Before long, it may fall to a "5" or a "2," or you may find you aren't recording an anxiety level any longer because it's at "0" and those negative thoughts that once triggered such a stress reaction have dissipated.

In some ways it seems almost like a miracle to me that an exercise like this, which is so easy to do, can produce such significant and lasting results. But it does. You just have to be a little patient, that's all. It's like an effective weight loss program with results that last versus a quickie starvation diet that leaves you packing on the lost pounds again in no time. Progress is cumulative, but before you know it—voilà!

Of course, you could stop right here, having already achieved a very desirable goal in itself—simple relief. But if your goal is more than just relief, if you want to win not just the battle but also the war itself, press on.

Exercise #3: Reframe

Now that you have identified and released the cause of the disturbance by bringing it to the surface, it's time to go on the offensive, because acknowledgment without taking action will not get you where you want to go.

Take that piece of paper with the line drawn down the middle, separating it into two columns, and print the following question at the top of the right-hand column:

"What I **want** to happen"

Now look over at your list of "worsts" in the opposite column and, one by one, reframe each negative expectation of what you fear might or will occur by turning it on its head to give it a positive outcome instead—in other words, what you *want* to occur (see figure 3).

Keep your positive outcomes performance-related. For example, if one of your top fears is being criticized in your job interview by getting turned down, instead of reframing the negative into a positive with "I want to get the job," which doesn't address the core issue, reframe it as: "I want to look calm and confident so that I will engage my interviewer."

If another of your top anxieties is that you will lose your place, instead of responding "I don't want to lose my place," say "I want to look confident and poised." And if you're afraid you will "go blank," instead of responding "I don't want to go blank," reframe the negative into a positive with a desired outcome that is more on-target, such as: "I want to handle all challenges gracefully."

Figure 3

The **worst** that could happen...	What I **want** to happen
lose place	I want to look confident & poised
go blank	I want to handle all challenges gracefully
be criticized **** embarrassed humiliated	look calm & confident
look foolish	I don't want to make mistakes

Once you have gone down your list of "worsts" that could happen and responded to each one with what you *want* to happen instead in the right-hand column, you will have an idea of each new possibility you are trying to create.

Now it's time to go one step further and create that possibility by affirming its outcome in the present tense.

For example, if in response to "lose place" in the left column, you wrote "I want to look confident & poised" in the right column, affirm that possibility simply by changing the sentence to read: "I AM confident and poised speaking in front of groups."

By affirming each "want" on your list in the present tense and writing it out on the page (see figure 4), you avoid falling into the trap of keeping yourself in a constant state of wanting (and, therefore, focusing on the future) rather than on having. You are focusing on achieving that outcome in the here and now.

Figure 4

The **worst** that could happen . . .	What I **want** to happen
lose place	I want to look confident & poised
go blank	I want to handle all challenges gracefully
be criticized **** embarrassed humiliated	look calm & confident
look foolish	I don't want to make mistakes
	Affirmations . . .
	I AM confident & poised speaking in front of groups
	or
	I AM a polished, confident speaker

Exercise #4: Visualize and Make Real

Okay, you have identified the underlying blockage, worked on releasing it, and reframed it to reflect your desired outcome. Now you want to turn that desire into a reality.

Ever since my years as an actress, a common technique I've used to achieve this is Visualizing. Here's the way my version of it works:

▌ Find a quiet place in your home, apartment, or office. Turn off the cell phone, radio, and/or TV. Sit in a comfortable chair. I recommend sitting up rather than reclining because as you go through this exercise you may start to feel drowsy, which is good, but I don't want you nodding off before you've completed the exercise.

▌ Quiet your mind and eliminate distractions. A technique that works well for me is: Picture yourself at the top of a long staircase. Now imagine descending that staircase, counting backward as you go down and breathing in the following manner. For example, let's say the staircase has fifteen steps. At the top step, count "fifteen" and inhale slowly. Exhale slowly. Next step, inhale slowly and count "fourteen." Exhale slowly. Next step, inhale and count "thirteen," and so on down the line until you have reached the bottom of the staircase in your mind's eye. If your mind starts to wander (and it might), don't pull yourself back to where you left off; ease back gently. The objective here is not to push or force your attention but to focus it so that you are able to slip into a deeper form of concentration.

▌ Having reached the bottom of the imaginary staircase, visualize entering a beautiful, serene setting that evokes in you a feeling of peace. It can be an environment that holds special meaning and pleasure for you, such as an idyllically deserted beach at your favorite lake, or a mountain trail where you love to go hiking. Or, it can be a totally invented spot—a land or seascape of your imagination where you fill in all the sights and sounds, as you desire. The objective is to create a peaceful space that you come to automatically associate with this exercise, where you can train your mind to go to quickly. After doing this a few times a day or a week, you will find yourself able to focus your attention and slip into that deeper state of concentration faster and faster.

▪ Now imagine your new possibility *in detail*. I love this part of the exercise! Let's say you have a presentation to your board of directors coming up, and the new possibility you have created and put in the present tense in exercise #3 is as follows: "I now look and sound confident and energized, and my presentation is well received." Visualize the event itself. Imagine yourself entering into the room, greeting the various board members, and delivering your presentation *as you wish it to be*. Likewise, visualize how you see the board members reacting to your presentation as you intend—i.e., responsively, enthusiastically, with applause, whatever you desire.

Alternatively, you might recall a past performance situation that was particularly successful for you and made you feel excited, elated, confident, on top of the world, or whatever. For example, that toast you made at your brother's wedding that went off especially well, or that presentation you made in the third grade that held the class enraptured. In other words, picture the outcome as you desire it. The more specific you are, the more powerful the suggestion you will implant in your mind and, therefore, the more likely the outcome will be exactly as you planned. Visualizing is not meant to be a substitute for a physical rehearsal of your upcoming presentation, of course. It is a support tool aimed at giving you the energy and focus you need in order to determine how much physical rehearsal you will need, according to your personality type and nervousness profile. It is a technique for putting yourself in a relaxed mental state, and one of the most powerful I know.

Be Careful What You Wish For, and Be Specific!

Here's what can happen when you're not specific enough. As an actress I once performed a staged reading of a new musical in which I had a small role as a comic French maid. Rehearsal was minimal, but that was standard for this type of money-raising venture, which is also called a backers' audition. The audience was composed of a lot of bigwigs in the business, and I was excited about the exposure but very nervous at the same time. Already familiar with the technique of visualizing, I decided to test it out in a performance situation and chose this one.

In my mind's eye I pictured myself entering the theater, doing "meet and greet" with some of the prominent cast and crew members I would be working with, going up onstage when it was my character's turn, walking to one of the music stands that would hold my script for the read-through, and gliding through my performance with panache. I even imagined the audience laughing at my character's antics. All of this may sound very specific, and it was, up to a point. The night came. Everything went almost exactly as I'd imagined it, until the moment arrived when I took my place at one of the music stands onstage to read my lines.

As I delivered them, I evidently pushed too hard on the stand supporting my script, and the stand dropped down, then down some more, then down some more, forcing me to lurch down onto my knees to keep reading. Everybody in the audience laughed. In fact, they howled with laughter. Unfortunately, it wasn't just my performance that tickled them, as I'd visualized; that damn music stand got into the act, too.

Whether or not the audience thought the whole thing was intentional, I don't know. But I knew it wasn't, and the embarrassment I felt led me to fine-tune my skill at visualizing *all* aspects of a performance situation, including the gaffes that can occur, so that in the future the laughs were definitely with me, not at me. It's amazing, but the more specific you are in imagining the details of your new possibility, the better able you are to spot potential glitches and solve them ahead of time, as you will already have identified and brought them to your attention!

Congratulations!

You have just completed the first and, in some cases, most important as well as most difficult part of your journey to becoming a natural and confident communicator: identifying the obstacle or obstacles standing in your way.

With surface obstacles like myths or skill-related roadblocks you have either dispelled them or now have a clear idea how to address them.

With murkier hidden obstacles that are more difficult to root out, you now have the tools you need to help you identify and release them.

Now you are ready to move ahead and develop a way of working that will help you create and deliver a powerful message.

So, don't touch that dial. The adventure continues!

PART TWO

Developing *Your* Way of Working

6

Bringing Your Message to Life

Recipe for Success

Let me share a story.

I was once the understudy in an off-Broadway show put on by Joseph Papp's Shakespeare Festival called *I'm Getting My Act Together and Taking It on the Road*. Like many acting hopefuls, I needed a supplementary job to support myself, and at the time, my day job was hostess at a restaurant in the Chelsea section of Manhattan.

It was not uncommon for me to work late into the night, then have to get up around the crack of dawn to get ready to hit the audition circuit. Looking back, I have no idea how I—or any of us, as I certainly was not alone—was able to do this, since a good night's sleep is so important yet was such a rare commodity. But passion, will, and discipline go a long way.

One night I arrived at my apartment around two A.M. completely exhausted from having worked at the restaurant. As was my custom, before falling into bed I would spread the tips I'd earned that evening out on the bed and tally them up to see if, together with my salary, I was accumulating enough to pay my bills that month, which included not just my living expenses but the costs of my acting classes and voice lessons.

As I counted the money out, I noticed a note on my pillow left by my roommate. The note said that Joseph Papp's office had called that afternoon asking me to come in to audition the next day for the road company of the show. I couldn't believe it! I wanted (needed) a real, honest-to-goodness, paying acting job more than anything else, and here was my chance! I practically danced on the ceiling I was so happy over this incredible stroke of good luck. But then it hit me: I was so excited, how would I ever get any sleep that night?

Somehow I managed to catch a few winks and was able to rouse myself in the morning, though I felt considerably less than fresh for such an important day. But at that point, I put my "system" to work.

I started with some warm-up exercises. Then I shifted to some stretching exercises. Then I went over some of my pre-prepared audition material, using vocalizing techniques that would not put too much stress on my vocal cords before the main event. And, finally, I visualized having a great experience at the audition, doing the best job I could possibly do that day. This is what my acting teacher kept telling me I should always aim for—because if I concentrated only on doing my best, I could let go of worrying about the results of the audition, which I had no way of controlling anyway.

I remember walking into the audition and, after the initial introductions, taking my place onstage and singing my piece. Typically with auditions there is silence afterward. But this time, the casting agent and one of the show's writers approached me and asked if I would quickly learn a song from the show with the accompanist onstage and give it a try—unfamiliar territory, but doable.

I did what they asked and gave it my all. And when I left that day, I knew I had landed the job of understudy for several roles, including the leading part. I also knew something else, something even more important: no matter how little sleep I got, or how exhausted I felt, or what unexpected challenge would come my way, I had a solid system that would always see me through.

The same principle applies to public speaking. If you have a system that you can apply over and over to see you through any circumstance, especially the most difficult, you may still get a case of the butterflies (as I do from time to time) when each new performance situation presents itself. But you will always have that system to get you through it.

I worked with a client who had recently become VP of a large pharmaceutical company. As he had not yet given a presentation in his new job, it was arranged for me to help him prepare for an important conference that was coming up.

At our initial meeting, he gave me a demonstration of the laptop presentation he had put together, which consisted of about sixty slides, many of them tables and charts full of tiny, unreadable print, as well other graphics he had pasted together. As he went through the presentation, he basically just read what was on each slide, speaking very, very quickly so as to cram all the information he had assembled into the twenty-minute time slot allotted him at the conference. As a result, he was unable to pause once to take a breath or ever look up at the audience.

When he finished, he asked for my reaction. "Do you think it would help if I asked them to give me a thirty-minute time slot?" he queried.

I replied that more time was not the issue. "The real issue," I went on, cutting to the chase, "is that I have no idea what your message is, no clear impression of who it's aimed at, and no clue why you are delivering it to this particular audience at this particular time."

I explained that the root problem was that he had no strategy in place for developing a message that reflected not only his interests and those of his company but the interests of his audience, as well. Furthermore, he had obscured his message with too much information. I also told him that a slide show is not a presentation, it is a slide show. Once a clear-cut message has been developed based on a well-thought-out strategy, then, of course, some well-placed visuals (in this case twenty at most) might be used quite effectively to support that message.

Many people I work with approach giving a speech, making a presentation, or preparing for an interview the same way this fellow did. Without knowing better, they throw ideas together into a big pot and stir. As a result, confusion sets in, and out of confusion grows anxiety.

Having worked in part 1 to identify and overcome what's been holding you back, your job now is to focus on the key elements involved in developing a successful communication.

Four High-Impact Ingredients

An effective speech, presentation, or interview cuts the fat, serving up a delectable platter an audience can digest and retain. It has the well-balanced ingredients of a gourmet meal, full of subtleties that tingle our taste buds. It is low in calories and high in fiber (substance), and presented in reasonable portions, infused with a few surprises that leave us feeling satisfied, energized, and with a desire to come back again sometime for more.

The most powerful and persuasive communicators use the following high-impact ingredients to drive their message home:

> *Define your objective* — specify the result you desire or action you want taken as a consequence of what you're communicating.

▌ *Know your ABCs*—understand the needs and concerns of the individual or group you're communicating to by developing an Audience-Based Communication.

▌ *Limit your message*—keep it simple and straightforward, and beware of the incredible expanding message! Does it match the needs and concerns of your listeners, or ask too much of them?

▌ *Create a structure*—establish a clear beginning, middle, and end to what you're communicating, balanced between data-driven information and anecdotal support.

These four key ingredients, when combined and allowed to simmer, will make your audience savor your message. Each ingredient is as important as the other. None should be left out. For Avoiders and Improvisers especially, learning to apply them may seem at first like an overwhelming task, but if you can withstand the heat and stay in the kitchen, you will find that in no time you are thinking strategically and assembling a recipe for redirecting your nervous energy into a usable approach that can be relied on time and again.

Let's take a closer look at each key ingredient.

1. Define Your Objective

Compelling communicators know whether to feed their audience an appetizer, a three-course meal, or a pig roast. So, the place to begin is with yourself—by defining exactly what it is you want your audience to feel, take away from or to do in response to your communication. In other words, start by asking yourself this: "Why am I here?"

I cannot stress strongly enough the importance of this first key ingredient. It is by not starting with it, or ignoring it altogether, that most public performances fail. Regardless of whether the communicator is experienced or a novice, here is where the communication can go immediately awry. There's an old Yogi Berra saying: "If you don't know where you're going, you'll wind up somewhere else." It's true. And, so will your audience!

After not defining an objective at all, the second most common mistake people make is to choose an objective that is:

a. Too big—it tries to accomplish too much at one time.
b. Unrelated to the task at hand—it is focused on a goal that is irrelevant to the communication or the situation.
c. Too murky—it is so nonspecific and, therefore, meandering that the audience or interviewer feels their time is being wasted.

Each of these mistakes can derail your message and squander your opportunity to deliver it ever again to that audience—or at least for a very long time.

Too Big

Steven was the president and CEO of a communications company that was on the cutting edge of designing Web sites and developing marketing strategies for major corporations in the early days of the Internet explosion. His company was so successful that IBM entered into an alliance with Steven's company as a business partner. As a result of this alliance, Steven was now expected to speak to potential customers at upcoming industry events.

Steven was in a panic when he came to see me. He was a "computer nerd" and graphic artist, he told me, not a public speaker. Even as the president of his own company he had never spoken to large groups before, and he was terrified—so terrified, in fact, that he was literally shaking before me at the thought of it.

"Okay," I said, "let's relax a little and go from there." Once he had, I asked what his objective was, what he wanted to achieve, at the first of these upcoming events.

Without a blink, he shot back, "My objective is to get a ton of business and impress the hell out of IBM!"

No wonder he was so nervous. He was setting very high expectations for himself and, therefore, putting tremendous pressure on himself to meet them. There was no way he could deliver an effective message from that perspective. And his focus was misplaced.

I asked him how many people would be attending the event. He told me seventy-five. I then asked how much new business one could realistically expect to gain from a single event such as this. "Oh, maybe five new accounts," he replied, with his feet now on the ground.

"Good," I said. "Now tell me what it is you want the other seventy people in your audience to do."

He thought for a second, then answered, "I want them to get excited about our business and file away in their minds for future reference how much we benefit the companies we work with."

"That's it!" I said. "Now you're on track. If you focus on that objective, you just might get those five new accounts (maybe more) *and* impress the hell out of IBM."

And the truth is, he did. The truth also is that he would never have delivered his winning message had he not focused on his audience's expectations and gotten specific about what he really wanted to accomplish.

Unrelated to the Task at Hand

A client of mine was preparing to give a status report on her department to the top management in her company. She was very tense about it and called me to help settle her down.

After observing her report (a long-winded and disjointed affair crammed full of detail about the various projects she and her staff were working on), I held up my hand and said, "Stop!" Then, I asked her what she was trying to accomplish with this report.

"I want them to see the value of my work, which has been overlooked up to now," she blurted, "and to give me that promotion I deserve but didn't get the last time." The resentment she felt at having been passed over was evident in her voice.

I was straight with her. "Wanting a promotion is not an objective," I explained. "It is a *desire*. It has nothing to do with the message you are delivering or why your audience should care to listen. Thinking that it does is only contributing to your anxiety." In the end, she realized that what she was really aiming for was to give her senior management a clear view of what her department was doing to grow its business, plus specific research-based recommendations of what she and her department could do to help management form even more successful strategies in the future. She delivered a message congruent with that objective, and, subsequently, she was rewarded for her efforts.

Too Murky

I once attended a lecture given by a woman about her recent trip to an exotic part of the world. Most of her comments about the journey were along the lines of how "interesting" it was and how "cute" the natives were. This may have been true, but such observations were so general, and her presentation so meandering, that I grasped no clear point from her, nor any rationale as to why she was giving this lecture to us in the first place. What was it that she wanted us to do—take the same trip? If so, why? Was there an especially educational aspect to visiting that part of the world? If so, what was it? Why was she standing at this podium in this building sharing her experiences with us in this particular group *at this time*? In other words, why did she think we either needed or wanted the information she was giving us?

If she had answered all these questions before stepping up to that podium, her lecture could, and would, have been a much better, more rewarding experience both for her and us. But as a consequence of not answering them, she lost her audience in the murk and her opportunity landed in the ditch.

Overall Objective vs. Specific Objective

Let's clarify some terminology.

If I were to ask you to define the objective of a football game, how would you respond—to win the game? Sure, that's the *overall objective*. But the more immediate, or specific, objective is to score the next touchdown, and the next, and the next—because that is how you'd reach your overall objective of winning the game.

Let's say your ultimate goal is to retire comfortably. To reach that overall objective, however, you must achieve a more immediate, shorter-term one, which is to set aside, say, $500 a month to fund your retirement plan. If you don't start with that, you will never reach your overall objective—unless, perhaps, you win the lottery!

The art (or, science, if you will) of communicating successfully in a public forum works the same way. If you were preparing for a job interview, how would you define the objective you want to achieve—as "Get the job"? Again, that may be your overall objective, but it is not specific enough to help you do the work necessary to put together an effective presentation that will set you on the path to achieving your overall objective and keep you moving forward so that you get there.

Here's an illustration of what I mean by the difference between overall versus specific objectives. I once worked with a daily newspaper that was trying to break into a new market in which the competition for advertising dollars was dominated by trade magazines. The competition was very stiff. The first time the reps went in to pitch a prospective company they came right out and asked for an ad placement *now*, as this is what they had defined as

FEARBUSTER

Forcing yourself to think strategically is one of the best things you can do to offset some of the ambient anxiety you may be dealing with in these early stages of preparation. By shifting your attention away from your personal concerns and onto the immediate task at hand—i.e., defining your objective, understanding your audience—you take the focus off whatever stress you may be experiencing and put it where it belongs. In other words, if you are thinking about what you really want to accomplish and devising a strategy for getting there instead of focusing on your anxiety, you are redirecting your negative energy on a positive course.

their objective. However, the newspaper did not yet have a track record, and so the prospective client did not yet perceive it as a player. They left without getting the business.

Obviously, the sales reps had to turn this perception around before they could even get close to scoring any advertising dollars from potential clients. Doing this meant homing in on a more immediate objective that, ultimately, would get them what they wanted. And so, they refined their objective from the more long-range "get clients to place ads now" to the more immediate "get clients to perceive us as players" that would ultimately lead to placing those ads.

Specificity is the key. The more specific you are, the more you increase your chances for success. Also, the more specific you are, the easier it will be to choose the right kind and amount of supporting material to help your audience understand and act on your message.

Different Stages, Different Objectives

In defining your specific versus overall objective, when asking yourself the question "What is it I want my audience to know or to do?" you must consider where you are in the process—because your specific objective will change depending on this.

Let's say you manage a company's sales force, and billing problems have arisen over time. To turn things around, you need to implement some strategic changes for which you require senior management approval. Several meetings have been scheduled over the next couple of days for you to make your case, first to senior managers in sales, then to the senior managers of other departments, and finally to the president and CEO.

Obviously, your overall objective is to convince management to give you the money and the support you need to implement your new sales ideas companywide. But if you go into the first meeting with "give me the money to make the changes" as your specific objective, you will likely emerge empty-handed. It's too much, too soon.

If you want to get anywhere, your specific objective for the initial meeting should be more like this: "Inform sales department senior management of the problems and issues involved in sales that are affecting the company." In other words, first get this group to understand what you say is happening and to sign on with your need for change.

Your next meeting is with the senior management of the other departments in the company. Here, your specific objective will likely become even narrower, as you have entered a different stage in the process. For example, it may boil down to "Secure recommendation to institute new sales program."

Finally, as you meet with the president and CEO and enter the last stage in the process of delivering your message, your specific objective will likely get even more tightly focused (as well as draw closer to your overall objective) and become: "Get budget approval for companywide sales initiative."

Here's another example, using a job interview situation.

Again, let's say several meetings have been arranged with your prospective employer. The first is with HR and the head of the department you would be working in. The second is with different department heads within the company. And the final meeting is with the CEO.

Your overall objective is to get the job—assuming it looks as good up close as it does from afar. But your specific objective might change as follows while you move through the process:

Meeting #1: "Determine whether the organization and I are a good fit."
Meeting #2: "Broaden acknowledgment that I'm the right candidate for the job."
Meeting #3: "Commit them to making me an offer."

Of course, you may get lucky and achieve all your objectives in one meeting by getting a job offer on the spot. But that seldom happens if you haven't defined your objectives in the sequence I've described so that your expectations going in are *realistic*. Expectations that are unrealistic (even if not out of the realm of possibility) produce anxiety, and anxiety decreases the chances of reaching any of your objectives.

Your specific objective is your guidepost. It helps you make clearheaded decisions about what—and how much—to include in or exclude from your preparation for each performance situation. Your specific objective is what takes your listeners a step forward each time, moving them ever closer at each stage of the communication process toward your bid for action. To keep the momentum going in the right direction, therefore, your defined objective at each stage must be specific to that stage.

Taking It up a Notch

When you ask yourself what it is that you want your listeners to know or to do as the result of your speech, presentation, or interview, you are basically determining how far you must shift them to get them where you want them to go—i.e., from *not knowing* → *knowing*; or, from *not doing* → *taking action*. This concept of determining how much and when to shift, or to move, the recipient of a message is understood and used by advertisers and marketing people every day in print, TV, and radio. The determination may be to shift your audience from one position to another in one seismic leap (perhaps to start placing orders for your products and services *now*) or by degree (at this stage, you just want to get your audience to start thinking about your company, its products, and its services in a different light). It is the *amount* or *size* of the shift you are asking your audience to make at each stage of the communication that signals whether your objective should change, to be sharpened or clarified.

Use Action Verbs

In defining your specific objective at each stage, use action verbs to powerfully describe what it is you are trying to do. Action verbs add punch to your message.

Even a speech or a presentation that is by design more informational in nature, rather than aimed at persuading listeners to act, benefits from the use of strong, action-oriented verbs in defining specific objectives at each stage. Let's say you have been called on to give senior management in the company an update on what's going on in your department, and you think, "Well, I'm just providing information." Nevertheless, that information has been solicited, and you are providing it, *for a reason*. Therefore, at the conclusion of your presentation, you will still want your audience to *do something* — even if it's just to understand, and feel confident, that things in the department are okay.

Spell out exactly what you want to achieve each step of the way. For example, instead of defining the specific objective of your speech to local school board members as wanting to get them to "consider an increase in the school budget," go for the bold and define it as wanting it to get them to "*commit* to an increase in the school budget."

In the case of interviews, devise objectives that help you actively demonstrate your capabilities. Instead of defining the specific objective of an interview with a prospective employer as "showing them how much I want the job," create a more appropriate and action-oriented statement such as: by the end of my interview the prospective employer will "*understand* how well I will fit into the organization."

In each case, the use of a more action-packed verb in the statement of your objective makes it stronger and clearer in describing what you really want your message to move your audience to do!

Try using action words like these to specify the objective(s) of your next speech, presentation, or interview. They'll add potency to your message:

- acknowledge
- implement
- develop
- increase
- sign on to

- know the value of
- change awareness of
- create a new
- adjust
- extend

FEARBUSTER

We all know that in the best of all possible worlds, nothing interferes with our plans and objectives. But, alas, this is not the best of all possible worlds. Stuff happens (i.e., the date of your pitch to potential investors suddenly gets shortened to a week closer, and your target audience shrinks by a third). You have to be flexible enough to be able to make adjustments accordingly. Because you are now thinking strategically, it will become much easier to roll with these punches.

2. Know Your ABCs

Just as a perfect hostess knows whether to serve dinner guests an exotic meal of Tibetan yak or simple American steak and potatoes, communicators must know their audience in order to deliver an effective message. This requires an intimate understanding of your listeners' needs and concerns—an understanding you acquire by investing some time analyzing your audience up front, and using the information you gather to tailor your message so that it speaks to the values and interests of that audience, thereby giving it a reason to want to hear you.

I call this ingredient creating an audience-based communication (ABC), and it is one of the fundamental yet most overlooked

FEARBUSTER

In the words of the founder of the National Speakers Association: "People don't care how much you know until they know how much you care."

ingredients in my recipe for getting and keeping your audience's attention. The best of the best know how to use this ingredient to make their performances soar and their messages hit the mark!

Knowing Your ABCs Builds Confidence

One of my mentors, the late Bill Gove of the National Speakers Association, once said to me, "Ivy, people get nervous over public speaking because they are *self*-conscious rather than *other*-conscious." He made an important distinction. By focusing all or most of your attention on yourself—"Will I stutter?" "Will they notice all the weight I've gained?" "Will I lose my job?" "Will they like me?"—you just increase whatever agitation you may be feeling, whereas by focusing on your audience, you make those nerves disappear.

This is the biggest self-confidence booster you can give yourself, because by redirecting your attention away from you, what *you* want, and how *you* feel, and putting it onto your audience, you are taking all that nervous energy that's building up and channeling it more positively into providing the best value you can to your listeners.

Of course it's only natural to want to be liked by your audience, your listeners, or an interviewer. Speakers who possess an innate quality of likability can gather a lot of support for their ideas, because other people tend to go out of their way to help someone they like. It's a natural instinct. However, the likability factor can wear thin if it isn't backed up by other qualities. It is more important—indeed critical—that they trust and believe you. And trust grows out of a feeling, communicated by you, that you are speaking to their concerns, that you have taken the time to understand what is important to them, and you actively demonstrate that what you have to say is significant and relevant to their situation.

For example, I observed a speaker recently who isn't especially likable, in the sense that he isn't blessed with the quality of personal magnetism that some speakers possess. He's quite tall, a little awkward, not particularly attractive, and has a raspy voice. But . . . when he gets up and speaks, he speaks firmly and so directly to his audience's concerns that he exudes self-confidence and is not only effective but also compelling. He is able to transcend his lack of charisma because he knows his ABCs. To achieve this, he employs the magic ingredient I call being an audience-based communicator.

Knowing Your Audience

As philosopher Robert Zend has wisely noted, "People have one thing in common, they are all different." The same is true of audiences.

For example, Philip, the senior vice president of a prominent financial firm, came to me for some tips on how to make his business presentations more compelling. His company's marketplace was global, and the competition was fierce, so he was constantly on the go having to speak all over the world.

He told me his problem wasn't that making speeches and presentations to large groups of people made him especially nervous, but that because competition was so tight, he needed a leg up: he wanted to be able to hold his audiences in rapt attention and put them in the palm of his hand, the way the best speakers can. "I want them applauding wildly at the end," he said. "How do I get that?"

Obviously, before I could make any recommendations, I had to analyze his current process for holding his audience's attention, so I asked him to give me a demonstration of one of his speeches, which went something like this:

"Good morning, I'm Philip. I'm the senior vice president of Ace Financial. In the next half hour, I am going to tell you all about

Ace Financial and the significant impact we have made in the global financial industry. At the end of the half hour, I think you will agree that we are the number one leader today in the financial markets we serve." Yada, yada, yada.

As he concluded his demonstration, he could tell from the expression on my face that he had a lot more work to do. I'll tell you why.

Let's take a pop quiz. Count how many times Philip used the pronoun "you" in this brief sample of one of his typical speeches to a group of business leaders and prospective clients. A grand total of twice.

Now count the number of times he uses "I," "we" or "I'm." Seven times!

This is a classic no-no. You can almost hear the audience responding to all those "I's," "we's," and I'm's" with a resounding "Who cares?" "What does this have to do with me?"

Philip was making a critical mistake in how he framed the information he wanted his listeners to hear and the message he wanted them to take away. He was presenting everything from his own rather than his audience's point of view. By framing everything that way, he was failing to demonstrate to that particular audience the value of hearing what he had to say and investing any amount of time listening.

I suggested to Philip that he take some time to ask and answer for himself the following questions about his target audience for this particular speech:

- Who were his listeners?
- Why were they coming to this event?
- What was important to them?
- What were some of the challenges they were facing?
- What level were they in their organizations?
- Was there anything they needed to learn to do better or differently?

▎ Was there anything he could offer them that they would consider new information?

▎ Where were they from?

▎ What was the male/female ratio?

▎ Were they a conservative group?

▎ Were they young, on the cutting edge?

▎ Was there anything he had in common with them?

▎ How much did they already know about him?

▎ How much did they already know about his topic?

Already he began to understand what I was after, because he realized now that he had never addressed most of those questions before, and the clear implication was that by not having done so, he was diminishing the impact he could have on his audience.

Philip followed my suggestions and reworked his speech. When he came back to give me a second demonstration, I knew within the first few seconds that he had undergone a major transformation in his thinking. Here's how it went:

"Good morning, I'm Philip. Before coming here today I had a chance to speak with some of you—Steve, Cindy, Todd—and I understand from them how concerned you are about growing profits in a business climate that is tough, competitive, and uncertain. Todd voiced the concern that the logistics are so tough overseas that it has become seemingly impossible to meet your goals. In the next half hour I will share with you some of the challenges we have recently faced at Ace Financial, and I will also share with you some of the strategies we have put in place to overcome those challenges that might work equally well for you. My hope is that you will take this information back to your companies and use it to create a competitive advantage in your own markets."

In these opening comments, and throughout the rest of the speech that followed, Philip always kept his audience in mind. He continually gave the audience a reason to keep listening to him by demonstrating the value of his message as it related to that audience. He was on his way to becoming a powerful presenter.

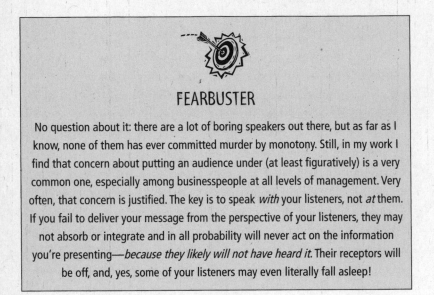

FEARBUSTER

No question about it: there are a lot of boring speakers out there, but as far as I know, none of them has ever committed murder by monotony. Still, in my work I find that concern about putting an audience under (at least figuratively) is a very common one, especially among businesspeople at all levels of management. Very often, that concern is justified. The key is to speak *with* your listeners, not *at* them. If you fail to deliver your message from the perspective of your listeners, they may not absorb or integrate and in all probability will never act on the information you're presenting—*because they likely will not have heard it*. Their receptors will be off, and, yes, some of your listeners may even literally fall asleep!

Ways of Studying Up

By taking the time to know your listeners, you build understanding, consensus, and confidence, and enter into a partnership with them where both sides win. There are many ways of conducting research and gathering the information you need in order to know your audience. Let's assume you are speaking before a certain audience for the first time—your board of directors, a prospective employer, or the Rotary club, for example. Here are a few idea starters.

▌ Talk directly to the person who is planning the event or meeting or their assistant if they're unavailable. Have a list of prepared questions.

▪ Ask for the names of prospective audience members and call a few ahead of time, if possible, to find out what's important to them and what challenges they face.

▪ Use the Internet to research the company, institution, or venue.

▪ Make use of the *Readers' Guide to Periodical Literature* and other microfilm or online databases available at your local library to look up magazine articles and newspaper clippings on the company, institution, or venue.

▪ Talk to someone who has interviewed with, presented, or spoken to the same individual or group.

▪ E-mail the company or institution for a copy of its annual report, marketing brochures, or business publications.

If all else fails (and most likely it won't), then get there early and glean some nuggets of information from the first to arrive by striking up a friendly conversation. This will allow you to make some on-the-spot adjustments to your speech or presentation, depending upon what you learn. For example, a woman came up to me after a recent one-hour program I was giving to her organization and shared with me that she recently found herself in a tough spot. She tried every avenue to reach members of her audience prior to her upcoming speech, to no avail. She prepared as best she could and then made a concerted effort to arrive early (actually the day before) at the event.

She struck up several conversations with attendees and gathered some valuable information. Through these conversations, she realized her audience was at varying degrees of understanding of her topic. Initially she had geared her talk to people who were very experienced in her field, only to find out that many attending this event were new to this industry. She realized that her new insights demanded an adjustment to her previously prepared remarks.

She revamped her original opening statements and started out by saying: "I had the pleasure of speaking with some of you this morning. My on-the-spot research revealed you have varying degrees of understanding of the topic I am addressing today. For those of you who are new, I'm going to spend a few moments and give you a thumbnail sketch on the background of our topic. If you find you still have further questions, please talk with me after and I can guide you to more comprehensive literature to help you fill in the gaps."

Knowing Your Audience May Change Your Objective

Preparing an effective message is a building-block process. The weight of each new block impacts the strength of the foundation with the new information it provides, which may force a change.

Once you feel confident that you have absorbed enough material to fully know your audience, go back and reexamine your specific as well as overall objectives. See if they still apply, or if what you have learned about your audience in the interim requires a change or shift in your focus. If so, it is certainly better to find out now, in the preparation stage when you can still do something about it, rather than later when you can't change the reality that you are putting together a meal of barbecued ribs for an audience of vegetarians!

3.   Limit Your Message

One of the worst aftereffects of overeating is how uncomfortable we feel. Information communicated the same way will produce the identical aftereffect.

A good speaker, presenter, or interview candidate doesn't overwhelm his or her audience with so much information that it cannot possibly be absorbed or retained. So, the third ingredient in your recipe for a successful communication is a limited and well-supported message that enables your audience to remember what you've fed them and act on it according to your wishes. In other words, you must trim off all the fat and serve up a lean and tasty entree your audience will savor.

A client of mine had to give an update on departmental progress to the president and CEO of his organization. I was invited to listen to a demonstration of the presentation and provide feedback. The presentation was to last twenty minutes and, in that time, cover all of the department's achievements (approximately fifty) over the past year, and go through each one. After the first few, I became distracted. After the tenth I found myself trying to keep my eyelids from visibly drooping. By the time the demonstration was finished, I had mentally itemized all of my Christmas gifts, birthday presents, and vacation plans for the upcoming year! It was impossible to remain engaged, and although the department had indeed accomplished much to be proud of, I had no idea what was truly important. The message was lost in the details.

I suggested to my client that he rethink his strategy and come up with a more creative approach that would highlight a handful of meaningful examples designed to make an impression and draw a big picture.

I am amazed at how many speakers, presenters, and job candidates drone on and on until their audience can't help but tune out from sheer self-defense. Conversely, audiences recognize and appreciate it when you clearly show that considerable effort has gone into creating a palatable but zesty speech or presentation.

For example, a client of mine in the advertising business asked me to work with his staff. I asked him what it was he wanted his staff to do differently, and, without missing a beat, he replied, "I want you to help them get to the point!"

He explained that his people were driving him crazy in staff meetings with their inability to present information and ideas to him in a clear, concise manner. "In addition to rambling on in a scattered, disjointed manner that seems to go on forever," he sighed, "they try to pack so much in that they get lost—or at least, I do!" This not only irritated him but also, in some instances, made him angry, because as a senior vice president in a fast-paced business, he has many responsibilities and limited time. It is important to him to be able to support his employees' ideas and interests, he said, "but they have to help me. I want them to know how to give me only as much as I need to know at that given time, and spell it out!"

Many of us are guilty of overloading the circuits of our audiences. I'm sure you have had the experience of sitting through a lecture or meeting or seminar and only minutes into it finding yourself checking your watch through glazed eyes, wondering, "When, oh, when will this be over?" and "Why am I here?"

Well, that is exactly what your listeners are thinking and feeling when you try to cram too much into an already scattershot and rambling message.

But please, don't be too hard on yourself. This is a common tendency for many people. We know so much about our particular expertise/subject/history, we think we must tell all we know or the other person won't get the whole picture.

Keep in mind that audiences today are raised on quick visual images. Attention spans are short, multitasking is routine, and we are trained to grasp information selectively. We are on information overload and cannot process, let alone remember, all that you may want to give us, which is all the more reason why you have to be selective and make it easy for us to digest your ideas.

It's also important to recognize that a spoken communication is much different from a written one. If I write a report and give it to you to read, you can take your time poring over it and rereading points for clarification. But with a spoken message, I have one opportunity to get my points across—and usually a limited amount of time to do it in. Therefore I have to design my communication so that it says in the given time frame what it *must* say, rather than all I may want it to say.

Serve Bite-size Portions

Brainstorming is a way of choosing and consolidating the most significant points in your message.

Let's say you have been given thirty minutes for your speech, presentation, or interview. As you brainstorm what to include and what not to include in your message, focus on distilling your message to three to five main ideas or essential points that will achieve your objective. To get there, ask yourself this about each idea or point you come up with: "Does it move my objective forward?" If you can't reply Yes right away, that point should probably be moved to the leftover pile. If you determine that you have, say, ten main ideas or essential points you want to cover, group them under three to five headings. The goal of the exercise is to eliminate anything that is irrelevant, confusing, redundant—or fattening.

Timing to Perfection

How might covering three to five main points in, say, a thirty-minute period look if you broke the session down? Here are two samples of the formula I use and recommend to my clients, which allow plenty of time to sufficiently address each salient point yet leave enough room for Q&A and/or dealing with the unpredictable.

Sample 1

Let's split the difference and say you have four main points or topic headings to drive home in order to achieve your objective:

Taking It up a Notch

Watch the pros and learn from them. Watch the network nightly news programs and observe how they tee up interest by telling you the three to five major stories or topics they will be focusing on in the next half hour, then move forward their objective of making you stay tuned by following through on that message. Similarly, the next time you hear a speaker, count how many ideas he or she incorporates in the speech. If the speaker was especially good in limiting his or her message, you should be able to remember those ideas with little difficulty, even weeks after the event.

Minutes per main point: 6 (× 4) = 24 minutes
Minutes for opening remarks: 1 = 25 minutes
Minutes for closing comments: 1 = 26 minutes
Minutes for Q&A: 4 = 30 minutes

Sample 2

Okay, let's go with the same number of main points or topic headings and the same thirty-minute period but say that you would feel more comfortable having more time for your opening and closing remarks and, especially, Q&A.

Minutes per main point: 3 (× 4) = 12 minutes
Minutes for opening remarks: 5 = 17 minutes
Minutes for closing comments: 2 = 19 minutes
Minutes for Q&A: 11 = 30 minutes

FEARBUSTER

When you limit your message, you show that you value your audience's time by wanting to make it profitably spent. This puts your audience on your side at the start so that you feel more at ease and, therefore, more confident of meeting your objectives from the get-go.

As you can see, these formulas are flexible enough to allow for any adjustments you wish to make. Use them as guides for breaking down your own message into scrumptious and easy-to-swallow portions. Determine what works best for your particular message and fits your particular comfort zone so that your servings will be timed to perfection.

4. Create a Structure

You know what your objective is. You understand your audience's concerns and desires. You've taken the time to limit your message to a few big ideas that your audience can grasp. What's next? You must organize your information or material and give it a direction that will lead to accomplishing your objectives.

Structuring how you will present your message is the bridge from the development phase to the delivery phase of the public speaking process. Structure is what enables you to operate efficiently under stressful conditions and make the right choices—those that will turn possibilities into opportunities.

Audiences also need structure. They do not respond favorably to a lack of organization on the part of the job candidate, speaker, or

👍

Taking It up a Notch

Are you familiar with this scenario? After spending days, maybe even weeks, of preparing for an upcoming sales meeting, client pitch, or job interview, you arrive on time only to be told by the person (or persons) you are scheduled to see that they are "so sorry" but they have to cut things short because they are being called away to put out a fire or something, and are in such a crunch that they can only give you five minutes. Your first impulse (after getting past the impulse to scream) is to suggest postponing the engagement to a more mutually convenient time. Your second impulse is to follow your original plan but to talk as quickly as possible and hope you can cram everything into five minutes. Which should you do? The answer is: neither. Ready a prepacked "fast-food" version of your entrée during your brainstorming session by asking yourself, "What would I include or eliminate if dinner plans turn to lunch instead?" In addition to making it possible for you to go with the flow so that you can still meet your objectives, preparing both a long and a short breakdown of the ideas and points you must cover, and how you will present them, will help facilitate, and even expedite, the process of identifying and eliminating the fat.

presenter. Their feeling is that if you haven't taken the time to adequately prepare for the interview, speech, or presentation, what on earth do they have to gain from hiring you, or listening to or acting on your suggestions? They decide on the spot that if you treat their time so cavalierly, chances are you approach the rest of your professional (and probably even your personal) affairs the same way.

Why You Resist

Even spending just a little time up front structuring your message makes all the difference between hearing comments like:

- ▊ "That was so easy to understand!"
- ▊ "She kept my attention throughout!"
- ▊ "Is it over *already*?"

And ones like:

- ▊ "I wonder what's on TV tonight?"
- ▊ "Maybe if I sneak out now, no one will notice."
- ▊ "Isn't it over yet?"

Nevertheless, people avoid spending even a small amount of time organizing and structuring their message. How come? Here are the most common excuses:

- ▊ *"I'm too busy. I don't have the time."* This is a common refrain, particularly among executives and other businesspeople. Sure, we're all busy, and getting busier, holding down two jobs, taking care of our kids, our parents, you name it. But be honest. Most of us waste an awful lot of time avoiding tasks and dreading events that we don't want to do or consider unpleasant. If we applied just a portion of the time and energy we waste with all that avoidance and dreading to structuring how we're going to present all that information swirling around in our brains, we would actually save time — and eliminate all that swirling, which contributes so much to our anxiety.

▌ *"I like to be free so I'll look and sound spontaneous and natural."* The only thing the "wing it" approach succeeds in making most of us free to look and sound is "disarrayed," "incoherent," and "stammering from nerves." This is the hit-or-miss school of excuses — the idea being that we might get lucky once, maybe even twice, and hit the mark without preparing. But that is a dismally low success rate, if you ask me. Speakers who look and sound spontaneous and natural come across that way

FEARBUSTER

Because there are so many things beyond our control that contribute to our anxiety in a public speaking situation, doesn't it make sense to do as much as possible to control what we can, as a tonic to that anxiety? As mentioned in part 1, I traveled around the country at one time in my career as a corporate spokesperson delivering company messages. It was not uncommon for me to travel to several cities each week, speaking at multiple events. Each venue was different from the next and presented me with new circumstances and difficulties that were beyond my control. For example, in one venue, the platform I had to speak from might be too high. In another, the technical crew responsible for running the audio and video equipment turned out to be even less savvy with gadgets than me. Or I might suddenly come down with the flu but still have to go on with the show. But no matter what came my way that was out of my control, I knew I could get myself back on track easily—and stay there—because I had created a structure for delivering my message that I could follow and that would always take me where I wanted to go.

precisely because they have organized their message. It's the application of a structure that enables them to achieve that look and sound.

▮ *"I don't know how to organize my message."* Okay, this excuse does have some degree of merit, especially with Avoiders and Improvisers, who, respectively, have never learned how to organize a speech or a presentation or prepare for a job interview because they steer away from any chance of being thrust into a performance situation or are put off at the thought of organizing anything, even their sock drawer.

▮ *"It's too hard."* What's hard is getting started. And that is hard only once. After you've done it and know how, structuring your message and how you will deliver it are a piece of cake!

The Perfect Blend

A good chef whets the appetite with an up-front delight that gives promise of what will follow, then adds some zesty spices to the main course and serves it up in an eye-pleasing manner, topping everything off with a mouth-watering dessert that not only completes the meal but also leaves a lasting impression.

Similarly, a good communicator structures his or her message so that it:

▮ prepares the audience to listen
▮ keeps the audience engaged and involved throughout
▮ helps the audience remember the message and act on it
▮ allows the communicator to stay flexible and be spontaneous

To achieve this perfect blend of positioning and persuasiveness in your speech or presentation, follow the basic outline format of breaking things down into a clear beginning, middle, and end—

a format that tells 'em what you're going to tell them, tells 'em, then tells 'em what you told 'em.

Your perfect blend will consist of the following elements:

1. A captivating opening, or introduction, and Audience-Based Objective, or statement of purpose, that promises and sets the stage for a positive exchange of information.
2. An engaging middle (or body) that is well balanced between data-driven information you want your listeners to know and anecdotal material with which they can identify and that memorably supports that information.
3. A strong close that moves your listeners to a specific response or action.

(1)   Create a Captivating Opening

Here is where you set the stage, just like the preview for an upcoming movie that draws you into the theater by providing the exciting highlights of what you can expect, and want, to see. You must bring your listeners on board and get them going in the same direction by preparing them for the journey they'll be taking with you, and laying out why that journey will be worth their time.

In a very direct sense, what you are doing here is establishing rapport—a connection between you and your listeners, some of whom you may be addressing, perhaps even meeting, for the first time.

When you are introduced to a person in a casual setting, typically you spend the first few seconds taking that person in and making some snap judgments about how you feel about him or her: like? dislike? warm? cool? friendly? or formal? Typically, this assessment occurs quickly and naturally. The same holds true for performance situations. Your listeners will size up you (and their feelings about you and your topic) immediately. By quickly establishing rapport, you give them right away what they need to make a positive assessment.

Rapport Needs to Be Genuine in Order to Be Effective

If you've ever encountered a pushy salesperson who tries to assume the role of your best pal the moment you meet, then you know what I mean by false rapport. It's not only annoying but also incredibly off-putting.

For example, my husband and I were in the market to sell a home recently. We had no idea what comparable property values were, so we arranged a meeting with a local real estate agent and asked her to research that information and to give us an assessment. When she arrived, she aggressively shook hands with my husband while ignoring me, then proceeded to make small talk with him, saying that she had known of his late father, who had been a prominent member of the community. As she finished, she looked at both of us and said, in all seriousness, "Good. We have instant rapport now!"

Obviously, she had read in a sales training manual somewhere of the importance of establishing rapport with one's customers, and really went by the book—because she then launched into a memorized spiel (it sounded that way) about how long her agency had been in business, how she was committed to selling our house, and so on. But when I asked her if she'd brought the information I'd requested, she had said she "forgot."

Instant rapport? There was no rapport at all! And there never would be, because not only hadn't she done what we'd asked her to do, she hadn't even done what she had said she'd do!

ELEMENTS OF A GOOD OPENING
The Grabber

If you can come up with a creative device to get your audience's attention and stimulate thinking right off the bat, so much the better—go for it. But keep in mind that your "grabber" must be appropriate to the occasion and tied to your topic.

A short story or anecdote that specifically relates to your topic gets you off to a powerful start and can help the audience get to know you. You can spice it up with some humor. For example, I once used a video clip* from the movie *Defending Your Life* to tee up my opening remarks for a presentation I called "Overcoming Fear and Loathing at the Podium." The clip showed the movie's main character, played by Albert Brooks, paralyzed with fright and sweating bullets backstage prior to giving a speech. I then followed the showing of the clip with the remark, "Does anyone else here feel this way, or am I the only one?" It was a light but provocative way of introducing the audience to me (and my sense of humor) and focusing them squarely on the topic.

Asking a hypothetical or factual question that requires a participatory response is yet another simple but effective tool for getting the ball rolling with your listeners. Let's say your topic is nutrition. You might open with, "Let me see a show of hands. How many of you use nutritional supplements? Now, how many of you use more than ten per day? Okay, what you are going to hear from me today may change the way you think about your nutrition and your health."

You can grab your audience's attention in any number of participatory ways—by asking some or all of the members to stand up; to say something; to think about something; to do something. Use whatever works for you. Just remember the main purpose behind it all, which is to take the audience's mind off whatever it was thinking about before you got up to speak, and bring it to the here and now of concentrating on the topic at hand.

*Be careful. To make use of any copyrighted material, such as a clip from a movie, in a public venue, you must get written permission from the copyright holder beforehand. As an alternative to going through that (believe me, it was a headache), I might have described the scene instead to my audience and concluded with the same remark. This would have been just as effective and required no permission, written or otherwise.

The Audience-Based Objective

Your Audience-Based Objective (ABO) is a statement that positions and frames your message from your audience's perspective. I always suggest to my clients no matter what type of communication you're delivering (with the exception of interviews), you want to focus your listeners with an idea that combines the *purpose* of the communication with the *benefit* to them. It gives your audience a reason, and the motivation, to listen to what you have to say. Whether you are delivering an inspirational message to your employees, asking for donations on behalf of your favorite charity, or giving a department status report, you must tell your audience what it stands to gain from spending the next few (or many) minutes listening to you!

Not offering this statement and just cutting to the chase by starting to talk is a crucial mistake. And some of the brightest, most senior people in business I've worked with have made it. They have taken for granted that just because they had the title or the prestige, they were in the driver's seat with their listeners, who would listen because they had to.

But isn't it better, and doesn't it get you farther, for your audience to *want* to listen to you rather than to have to?

Taking the time to craft your Audience-Based Objective in your opening remarks makes a significant difference in how your audience will respond to you and to your message. It is a powerful and persuasive tool no matter what venue you are in.

Let's say you are asked to inform the employees in your group of the safety measures necessary to follow in case of a fire alarm. Instead of just opening up with, "Here's what to do in case of a fire alarm"—which most of us would tune out because our tendency is always to think: "What do I need to know that for? It'll never happen to me"—give some thought to what they will actually stand to gain from that information, and tell them. For example, your ABO might be: "I'm going to take you through the ten steps in our fire alarm procedure so that you will understand how each step works, but more important, how they work together to save your life."

If you precede or follow your Audience-Based Objective with a personal experience of yours, or an experience of someone you know, who found himself or herself in a situation where knowledge of this information did indeed spell the difference between life and death, you will have captured your audience's attention with a definitive "what's in it for them" that they will retain.

The only situation to which this doesn't usually apply is the interview. The interviewer usually initiates and directs the conversation in the beginning. It would sound too formal and stilted to begin an interview by saying: "In the next twenty minutes I am going to demonstrate the added value I bring to you specifically as a potential candidate for the job in this department—and to your organization as a whole as a prospective longtime employee." Your interviewer would probably roll his eyes and prepare to settle in for the long haul! In an interview, you can lead into areas of discussion, in response to a question like: "Why do you think you are right for this job?" and other questions along those lines, with reinforcing phrases such as: "I think I would be a good fit for this particular job because I work well under pressure. In college I often juggled several tasks simultaneously. For example . . ."

The Preview Statement

When you are driving your car, you don't make a turn without signaling (at least you shouldn't!). Otherwise, you might cause an accident and hurt yourself or someone else. Same thing applies here. You must give your listeners an idea of the direction you will be taking them so as not to lose them or cause a mental pileup by making an unexpected turn.

The preview statement is a technique for doing this. It briefly summarizes up front what you are going to talk about, and how

FEARBUSTER

In every performance situation, one third of your audience will be instantly predisposed to liking you. Another third may not have an instantly favorable reaction to you for reasons totally beyond your control, such as your coincidental resemblance to a disliked brother, aunt, or mother-in-law. The last third will be on the fence and can be swayed either way. By establishing rapport, clearly indicating where you will be taking everybody and the value of going there with you, you can push that neutral third over to your side quickly. Once you've got 66 percent in your corner, there's a good chance others will follow, even if you do remind them of their in-laws!

you intend to proceed in your discussion, so that your listeners know where you will be taking them and will be able to follow.

Your preview statement can be as simple as: "Today I'm going to talk to you about our new project: where it stands today, how it got there, and where it is going in the coming months." Or: "Today I'll be addressing A, B, C, and D. But I'm starting with D because I know that's uppermost on your minds. Then we'll go back and look at A."

An opening statement that grabs, an Audience-Based Objective that demonstrates the value of listening to you, and a preview statement that points your audience toward the light at the end of the tunnel—these are the elements you must understand, and use, to set the stage properly for yourself *and* your audience, if you wish to become an effective communicator.

(2) Create a Middle That Balances Data-Driven Information and Anecdotal Support

If a recipe calls for two tablespoons of curry powder and you add one cup, you are in danger of sending your gourmet meal down the drain and your dinner guests for the water jug. Public speaking works the same way.

The body of your communication puts forth the key ideas or messages you want your audience to take away and act upon. Therefore, you must ask yourself, "How can I present them in a way that is both credible and memorable?" The answer is to balance the nuts-and-bolts data (statistics, factual evidence) in your case with enough anecdotal support material (examples, personal stories, analogies) to engage and convince your listeners so they'll want to remember and act upon what you've told them.

Not every member of your audience will process information the same way you do. If you are an analytical person who gets turned on by data and who leans heavily toward a "just the facts, ma'am" approach in your speeches or presentations, blending some anecdotes into all those facts (and figures and pie charts) will go a long way toward reaching your *entire* audience. Conversely, if you are a great storyteller and lean heavily toward anecdotes in your communications, be sure to blend in some data as well to strengthen your credibility and reach the facts-and-figures segment of your audience.

Let's say you are being interviewed for a job that requires a lot of teamwork. After you have captivated your prospective employer with a successful opening, it all goes downhill if you follow that with something like: "I am a very good team player. I played a lot of sports in college and we never lost a game. I really like being part of a team." Boring.

At this stage, your message calls for some well-rounded elaboration in order to drive it home. The way to achieve this is to provide some actual statistics relating to what you've cited, and to tell exactly how you functioned as part of the team to score those great statistics. In addition to presenting your case in a more interesting and memorable way, you will likely summon up the same energy and enthusiasm you felt as part of the team, resulting in a clearer picture of the real you.

A friend of mine in human resources confirms this. "The importance of the anecdotal reinforcement of your message in an employment interview, a staff meeting, or any other job situation where you are presenting a lot of [dry] data, is critical," she says. "For example, after interviewing the candidates for a job opening, all the decision makers, like myself, go behind closed doors to discuss them and make the final selection. Invariably, the candidate we most often get behind and offer the job to is the one who stands out most in terms of having painted the clearest, most vivid picture of his or her qualifications with memorable anecdotes that supported that picture. I know that's what makes me want to go to bat for that person."

Tell Stories

I have discovered through my own experiences as a public speaker that people will remember a well-told story related to a point I've made in a seminar or other speaking engagement for a long time. In some cases, they've come up to me years later and said, "I am still thinking about that story you told! Every time I get into a particular situation, I am reminded of that story." What they are really saying is: they are reminded of the point I was making, which that story I told supported.

Because they do it for a living, professional speakers know where to draw stories from and how to craft them, even using acting techniques to bring their stories and messages to life. They also hone these skills continually by seeking out and crafting new stories to keep their speeches and presentations fresh, and to prevent themselves from growing stale. However, you don't have to be a professional speaker to put their techniques to work. Just learn the basic principles of good storytelling and insert some stories relating to your topic or message into your next public speaking event, job, or college interview:

CRAFTING YOUR STORY

A quick and easy way to remember the principles of crafting a story so that it (and your message) comes alive for your audience is to think of the word CORE, an acronym I've come up with that stands for the following:

Characters and Conflict—Set the stage by introducing and describing the characters in the story, and the conflict(s) they must deal with and triumph over, as relating to your message.

Obstacle Overcome—Show how the characters approached whatever obstacle they were facing in an effort to overcome it.

Resolution—Tell your listeners how things turned out.

Ending—Tie the resolution, positive or negative, back to the main point, main idea, or main objective of your message.

This same concept can also be used effectively to craft stories in a job interview or sales situation. Let's look at a typical interview scenario. One of the most common things a job candidate is asked to do in an interview is describe a problem, work-related or otherwise, that he or she had to overcome. Let's say you respond with the recollection of how, having just graduated from high school at seventeen, you needed to get a summer job to help pay for your college tuition. As you had no job experience at all, you had to really put your thinking cap on in an effort to convince prospective employers why giving you a chance was to their advantage.

You explained that what you lacked in experience you made up for in industriousness, ingenuity, and team spirit and gave an example of how you applied those qualities to making good on your high school soccer squad. As a result, you got several good job offers that summer, not just one, and emerged a seasoned pro. Today, you still apply the same principles of industriousness, ingenuity, and team spirit to every new job challenge you face.

Interview Situation

Character and Conflict: You, a high school graduate of seventeen, needing a job to pay for college.

Obstacle Overcome: No experience.

Resolution: What you did to convince prospective employers to give you a shot, and how you emerged a seasoned pro.

Ending: The point that as you apply the same principles to your work habits today, it's to this new employer's advantage to give you a shot at the job, as well.

Now we'll apply CORE to a sales situation.

Let's say you are pitching your services to a customer who has a particular business problem. You tell how you had another customer with the same (or similar) problem and describe in detail, using all the color and imagery you can summon, how your service exceeded the customer's expectations in solving the problem and made him or her deliriously happy. Then you make the point that if your service solved that problem so successfully, it can solve this customer's problem with the same high degree of satisfaction, too.

Sales Situation

Character and Conflict: The customer with a business
problem that needs fixing.

Obstacle Overcome: The problem (what's broken and
the damage it's causing to the business).

Resolution: The application of your service to another
customer's similar problem and degree of success and
customer satisfaction in making the problem go away.

Ending: The point that your service can provide the
same successful solution and bring the same level of
satisfaction to this customer, too.

WHERE TO GET STORIES

Here are some idea starters to help you come up with other
possible sources for story material on your own:

a. Your daily routine. Ever come home from a long, hard day at
work and said to your spouse, partner, or roommate: "You
are not going to believe what happened to me today"? You
then unfold a tale about the idiot in the cubicle next to yours
who spent the entire day interrupting you with stupid questions as you were rushing to meet a deadline—and you
couldn't shut your door on him because you don't have one!
That kind of slice-of-life incident from a person's daily routine is something we all can identify with and might make for
a light but to-the-point story for driving your related message home.

b. Lessons learned. Recall valuable lessons you have learned
from challenges you've faced and successes you've achieved

in your personal or professional life and apply them to business. Perhaps it was an important lesson you learned from a great teacher; your minister, rabbi, or priest; a coach; a particularly difficult taskmaster of a manager you once worked for; someone you worked with who made a lasting impression because of their work ethic; or how someone you know managed to overcome a setback. If so, tell how and why the lesson was worth learning. Then tie that lesson into your message.

c. General observations. Be observant. Keep track not only of the trials and tribulations you experience throughout each day as fodder for stories, but also the offhand comments, routine activities, and daily trials and tribulations of your spouse or partner, your kids, your friends, and coworkers, as well.

If you are afraid that you will forget a story you thought of by the time you have to put together your next speech or presentation, do what professional writers and speakers do: keep a notebook with you at all times—even on the nightstand beside your bed. When a story comes to you, jot down the details in the notebook. That way, you won't even have to think about remembering them afterward and won't risk losing the opportunity to enhance your message with that story.

USE ANALOGIES

Analogies can provide powerful anecdotal support to your message, because they can help your listeners grasp a complex or unfamiliar idea by putting it in layman's language or terms they can understand more easily.

For example, a client was recently promoted to a position that required her to do a lot of public speaking. She was nervous because she was unskilled and thus had very low expectations of herself. Her speaking style was stilted and lackluster, and her content was fact-driven and noncompelling.

I asked her if she had any hobbies. She said she loved to play golf. I've never played golf myself, but I've seen enough of it on television to at least know who Tiger Woods is, so I asked her to explain to me what I would have to learn to be able to play the game. She answered, "You would have to focus on three things: your stance, your grip on the club, and your swing. When all those are in sync, you're on your way to being a good golfer."

Coincidentally, the topic of her upcoming speech had three key elements to it as well—design, technology, marketing—that, when integrated, significantly impacted performance. In that respect, her presentation's message of the whole being greater than the sum of the parts was not unlike what she'd told me about golf. I felt it reasonable to assume that many in her audience would be golfers, or at least familiar with the sport like me, so I suggested that she work the analogy into her speech—and support it with personal anecdotes about her own experiences on the course and observations about the world of golf at large that tied into her subject and data. She did and scored a hole in one. Not only did her presentation come alive and stick with her audience, the speaker who followed her revised his prepared opening on the spot to continue her golf analogy in describing his part of the process under discussion.

Use Transitions

One of the main reasons people stutter and stammer and get sidetracked and confused or lose their audiences in a performance situation is because they don't build transitions into their communication. Using simple transitional phrases like "We've talked about X, now let's look at Y," or "We all have a pretty good idea how we got here, let's see where we're headed next" will help guide you and your listeners seamlessly through your speech, presentation, or interview.

Come up with a list of transitional phrases of your own. Nothing fancy, just simple transitions like the ones I've illustrated.

Taking It up a Notch

A meal that is presented well—that is to say, looks good in addition to tasting good—is more satisfying all around. But the presentation must complement the meal, not overwhelm it. It's the same with public speaking. Remember the adage Less is more. Laptops, PowerPoint displays, and myriad other wonderful gadgets and gizmos exist to provide visual impact to our speeches, presentations, and interviews—and I encourage using them but not to the point of distracting the audience from your message with a lot of needless razzle-dazzle. With all due respect to the late Marshall McLuhan, here the medium is not the message; your words are.

Write them on the pages of your speech, the outline of your presentation, or prep sheet for your interview where they'll be used, and relegate to the past those irritating nonword transitions like "um," "ah," and "er" that make us squirm as listeners and as speakers.

"HUMANIZE" YOUR MESSAGE

I used to refer to this as "personalize your message" but rephrased it because some clients, especially business executives, interpreted it to mean sharing personal information suitable only for a doctor's office or a psychiatrist's couch. They shy away from it. So, now I use the word *humanize* instead. But whatever word this concept goes by, it's a powerful one for communicating your authentic self—because it gives what you are saying an experiential, personal twist that will make it more meaningful to your audience.

A great example of how to humanize a speech successfully was demonstrated by a client of mine, the president of his own company, whom I'll call Brad. He had to deliver some difficult speeches to his employees around the country. The business climate was tough. There would be job cuts and a complete reorganization of the company; its remaining employees would be called upon to do more with less. Sound familiar?

It is typical of companies in such situations to deliver bad news like this in a canned manner that often comes off to employees as patronizing and gratuitous—delivering a message in a way that appears it doesn't really care about employees' feelings.

But Brad was a good leader and really did want his people to feel they were part of a culture that cared about them. Plus, he truly enjoyed speaking and was quite good at it—or, at least, better than many CEOs I've seen. However, his attempts to inspire and motivate were not really getting through, and he was not connecting with his employees on the level he sought.

Since Brad's goal was to motivate his employees to work harder, in spite of the significant stress to their professional and personal lives that the company's belt-tightening cutbacks would cause, I began by asking him this: "Who in your life instilled in you the values and work ethic you embody? In other words, whom do you think of when times are tough to motivate you to work just a little bit harder?"

The answer was his grandfather. I asked him to tell me about his grandfather, and he unfolded a beautiful story that evoked in me familiar images of my own grandfather, who had come to this country and worked under impossible conditions, enduring indescribable hardships day after day, but survived and laid the foundation for all that I am and enjoy today. This was the work ethic Brad wanted to inspire in his employees—and the perfect story to support that aim, since most of his employees would likely be able to identify with that story and respond to it as I did, which was exactly what he was trying to accomplish.

Though still a bit reluctant to be so self-revealing, and with a healthy dose of skepticism over whether it would work anyway, he crafted the story about his grandfather into his speech. The day after he gave the speech, I received a phone call from him and knew in a second from the excitement in his voice that he had hit a home run. He said he'd never had such a response from *any* speech he'd given. People just wanted to come up to him afterward, shake his hand, and relate stories about their own grandparents to show how onboard with him they were. Mission accomplished.

Look for opportunities to humanize your speech or message— yes, even in a business setting!—and you will reach your listeners on a deeper, more emotional level, one that succeeds in motivating them to help you achieve your objectives in ways you've never experienced before.

Some people believe humanizing the message means having to step out of their comfort zone and be something they've not, like touchy-feely or flashy and outgoing.

For example, Gerard, I'll call him, is a brilliant man with an engineering background. He rose to a top spot in the financial division of his company because of his analytical abilities and business savvy. Highly educated and sophisticated, he disapproved of any overt display of emotion or false bravado in his behavior.

His manager asked me to work with Gerard, who had been given the task of speaking at a combined conference of the company's finance and sales people about the new direction the company was taking. As Gerard was the financial guru who'd put together the partnerships and affiliations that would be instrumental in taking the company in its new direction, he was the natural choice to sell the idea to the conference's diverse constituencies.

The problem was, Gerard was a thinker, not a relater—he was all about the nuts and bolts and expected the audience to be the same way. In other words, his approach was entirely self-directed, not other-directed.

I suggested the need for some energy and commitment in his delivery style. He disagreed. He said he had no intention of going in that direction. It would be phony for him to do so, he told me.

I clarified that it wasn't necessary for him to act like a clown to make his audience sit up and pay attention. But being more animated would go a long way toward successfully putting his message across to his diverse constituencies (which, bottom line, was key to achieving the company's goals).

There are ways of speaking to an audience, I maintained, that would make him become more animated without suffering any loss of dignity. And one of them—a *big* one—was not to adopt the typical "take-it-or-leave-it/just-business/one-size-fits-all" approach.

After much discussion, I got him to see the validity of my point, which is to talk *with* your audience (i.e., from its perspective) rather than *at* your audience (i.e., only from yours). He agreed that if he approached the speech his way, he might keep the finance people involved but would probably lose most of the salespeople to repeated bathroom breaks.

"Okay, let's develop something that speaks to both factions," I offered. The World Series games were in progress, so I asked him if he liked baseball.

"No," he answered. "I'm only interested in soccer."

"That's great that you're interested in soccer," I said. "But your salespeople probably aren't and neither are your finance people—at least not now. They're all watching the World Series."

I gave him a homework assignment. I told him to watch that night's game and work on some baseball analogies for his talk. He wasn't too sure about my plan but went along with it anyway.

Rehearsal day arrived, and I asked him what he thought of the game he'd watched. "Great!" he said, adding that he'd watched the rest of the games as well. "How about that pitcher?" he said. "And that triple play was fantastic!" He was really into it, and it showed.

At the conference, he opened by making an observation about the World Series. The audience loved it. Then he wove in an analogy between the company's objectives, the games, and the performance of that particular pitcher into the speech that everyone in the audience related to. As the audience responded, he became more energized and engaged, and his audience did, too.

This was quite an achievement for such an introverted gentleman. He'd gotten his first taste of how to be engaging and human without having to step too far out of his comfort zone. He was well on his way.

Taking It up a Notch

Rediscover the talents you have let grow idle or things you once loved to do and have either lost touch with or forgotten—and use these aspects of yourself to bring greater authenticity and power to your message. For example, I once heard an engineering executive describe an intricate technical application in musical terms by likening the developing of the application to writing a symphony (which he had actually done at one time, because music was his hobby). The audience was riveted because he had tapped into and conveyed a unique part of himself and his creativity that both deepened his listeners' understanding of the application itself and developed in them a greater appreciation for him, his talents, and the credibility of his message.

(3)   Develop a Strong, Clean Close

In the theater, a good drama always comes to a powerful conclusion, and a good comedy "always leaves 'em laughing." So, don't end your speech, presentation, or interview with "Phew, glad that's over!"

Having steadily moved your listeners toward your specific objectives throughout your speech or presentation, now is the time to take them over that goal line to your overall objective. If you are being interviewed for a job, perhaps it's to make you an offer. Or, in another type of situation, you may want them to increase your budget, or agree to join the Thursday night bowling league. Whatever your overall objective is, you have a couple of ways of closing that will achieve it:

You may either cap things off by summarizing the main ideas you have discussed and reiterating your Audience-Based Objective as a nudge or form of friendly persuasion. Or you can ask for a specific action to be taken and even suggest the next step.

Whichever form of closing you choose, remember that its purpose is to bring your speech, presentation, or interview to an end strongly and, most important, *cleanly*. In other words, don't leave your listeners hanging, wondering what to do with the information you gave them or what they just heard. You want them to know what you want them to do after they leave, and then to do it. But for that to happen, you must know, as well. So, in a sense, you end where you began—by asking yourself, "What do I want them to do?"—and revisiting your answer in your close.

Voilà!

You know your objective. You know your audience. You have used that knowledge to create an audience-based communication in which you have limited your message to make it easily digestible. You have created a workable structure for your speech or communication that will help keep you and your audience on track and engaged. And you know what spices to add that turn a so-so dinner into a gourmet delight. In short, you have finally started thinking strategically and are over the major hurdle to achieving your ultimate goal.

Now let's take a look at the physical skills you will also need to inject that factor into your public speaking life.

7

Doing What Comes Naturally: the Five Physical Skills That Get You There

Not a "Natural" Situation

Whether you are standing at a podium, seated at a conference table, or being interviewed over lunch in a "relaxed" atmosphere, speaking before a group of people (large or small) is not a natural situation. Unlike the casual communications we partake in every day with friends, colleagues, and family that may cause us to feel some stress as well, professional or formal speaking situations take that stress to a whole other level.

Sure, you know how to talk and to move. But even so, as soon as you are asked to step up and say a few words, or you hear your introduction ("Ladies and gentlemen, give a warm welcome to Steve S. from *Mainstream* magazine"), or you take your seat for that all-important job interview, you are "on." And as the self-assured, easygoing person you normally are turns into a sweaty, clammy, uncoordinated klutz that even you don't recognize, you find that what works for you in suppressing stress in everyday

communicating isn't sufficient to get you through these more har-
rowing situations in the spotlight.

The good news, though, is that as you learned in the last chapter, once you have a way of working—in this case, solid techniques and skills at your disposal for physically delivering your
message—you can alleviate much of that stress, or at least better
control its physical, mental, and emotional toll on you. Furthermore, these techniques and skills will also enable you to develop a
natural delivery style that allows you to communicate in ways that
reflect who you really are—authentically and with confidence.

A Solid Foundation

Honing your presentation style is like learning to play a musical
instrument. No matter what instrument you play, it's a good idea
to start with a classical foundation. To play the guitar, for example, you must first learn the finger positions; then you must practice them over and over until you no longer think about them as
you play. As these actions become integrated and ingrained, they
just happen automatically. You are now free to interpret a piece of
music however you want, so what emerges is a form of expression
that is more artistic than formulaic, and unique to you.

The same is true of public speaking. Building a solid foundation
by learning basic physical skills helps you manage the pressures
of various communication situations and then sets you free to add
the nuances that ultimately define your authentic style.

The goal in this chapter is to teach you the five physical skills
that will enable you to redirect your energy to achieve an animated
and engaging delivery style that is authentic to you—in other
words, a delivery style that speaks to your audience in a manner
that is congruent with your personality because it is based on the
real you and thus is credible to your audience. If you're not a high-

energy, dynamic, motivational individual one on one, chances are you're not that kind of a public speaker either, so don't try to become one. But perhaps, in the manner of a teacher, you like to tell stories that offer lessons. If so, you should use that as the basis for your delivery style because it is natural to you.

For example, a gentleman I worked with is the vice president of a major corporation. He's in the public eye and gives speeches often. One on one he was quite warm and engaging. But at a conference where I saw him speak, he exhibited a complete lack of the warmth and personality that he showed in person. His delivery style was totally flat, which was typical in these situations, he told me.

I asked him when he felt the most comfortable and the most effective communicating with people. He replied that this was when he was mentoring and coaching his employees. So, I suggested that he tap into that part of himself when he had to make his next speech.

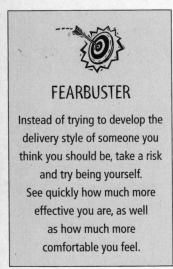

FEARBUSTER

Instead of trying to develop the delivery style of someone you think you should be, take a risk and try being yourself. See quickly how much more effective you are, as well as how much more comfortable you feel.

He worked with this concept, along with some additional tips I gave him, and in a very short time developed into a warm and engaging public speaker who came to enjoy the process of coaching and mentoring his audiences as much as he did coaching and mentoring his employees, thereby boosting his self-confidence as a speaker and increasing his impact on his listeners. This is because when he speaks now, he speaks from both his head and his heart. His listeners know they are in the presence of an astute businessperson, but at the same time he exhibits the warmth and personality of a favorite teacher and makes them feel he cares. This is a powerful combination.

Matter of Degrees

Once we find our authentic delivery style, it stays with us, becoming automatic. All we do after that is make small adjustments of "more" or "less," depending upon the venue—e.g., addressing a large audience from a stage, presenting to a small group from a conference room chair, or being interviewed on television as a spokesperson for a company.

For example, when I give a seminar in a classroom-size venue, my style of delivery is at one level, but when I work in a large auditorium with a bigger audience, that venue requires me to up my delivery style by increasing my vocal projection, enlarging my gestures, and so on. It is necessary to do this in order to reach the people all the way in the back.

Conversely, on video or television I have to tone everything down, because the camera magnifies everything, especially movement, and a gesture that is already broad may look too exaggerated.

Once you master the basics and you adjust according to the required setting, you then set the stage for individual interpretation that is the cornerstone of authentic speakers.

Like a River

Many of us do not understand how our bodies work under pressure in such situations. We think of ourselves as just being excited or nervous, whereas what is happening to us is actually physiological in nature: a surge of excess energy flows through our bodies from the release of the hormone adrenaline, brought on by our emotional state. If we don't have a way of releasing and channeling that excess energy so that it flows evenly and naturally in a positive, productive direction, it may explode from us, throwing us into overdrive, or implode on us, creating inhibitions. Either result may manifest itself in certain physical characteristics that will impede our best presentation performance and/or distract the audience's attention from the message we are trying to communicate.

For example, an explosion of excess energy may result in chaotic, uncontrolled movement or other nervous behavior that fixes the audience's attention entirely on the tic rather than the topic. Conversely, when we repress the flow of excess energy and cause an implosion, we may exhibit a different kind of physical behavior, such as shaky legs, twitching and sweaty hands, dry mouth or throat, a tendency to rock back and forth (or sideways), or speak too softly, that is equally distracting and counterproductive.

Energy is like a river, constantly in motion—even when calm. Obstruct a river and the water doesn't stop moving. It just changes the way it moves. If you try to dam the river without creating a spillway for controlling the release, the banks may overflow and the land will be flooded. In public speaking situations, as pressure builds and you feel the surge of excess energy it creates, you must be able to physically control the movement of this energy so that it is released outwardly, through the communication—thereby adding to the communication's strength—and not inwardly, jeopardizing the communication.

Since energy is such a key component of a successful speaking style, it's important to observe how professional speakers and communicators control its release and use it to create an ebb and flow that pulls their audience toward them rather than away. For example, a client of mine named Barry loves to speak. He can't wait to get out there and get going. He hits the ground running, peppering his audience with questions, tapping every ounce of his souped-up energy to foster a dynamic image and generate excitement in his audience. But what he comes across as is a fast-talking salesman on a late-night infomercial, and although he may have been enjoying an adrenaline rush, his viewers wanted to change the channel. He needed to better manage his energy and let it build from a powerful but controlled start so as not to overwhelm his audience.

To achieve this, you must understand and work on the five physical skills that will get you there. They are:

1. *Balance*—distributing your weight to achieve and maintain a natural, comfortable position when standing or seated
2. *Breath control*—breathing deeply to keep anxiety at bay, yet not too rapidly, so as to avoid nervous hyperventilation
3. *Eye contact*—talking with your audience, not at them
4. *Hand placement and gestures*—animating and energizing your message comfortably
5. *Vocal power*—adding energy and authority to your natural voice

Mastering each of these five skills will enable you to better control the flow of excess energy that can contribute to anxiety, and enable you to become the best communicator you can be.

Physical Skill #1: Balance

How to Stand

I watched a client in one of my seminars recently get up to demonstrate how she would give a speech. She crossed one foot over the other and started talking, completely unaware that she had twisted the lower part of her body into a pretzel and frozen the upper part by clasping her hands tightly behind her back. She reminded me of an unhappy five-year-old forced to stand at the front of the class, not the business professional that she was.

When I asked why she had positioned herself this way, she explained that she was used to speaking at staff meetings and similar situations where she would be seated around a conference table, and felt comfortable sitting. Giving a speech or a presentation standing up made her feel vulnerable, so she guessed she had assumed the position she'd taken in order to make herself feel less exposed and safer.

Ballet dancers begin their training by learning the basic positions from which all movements and steps follow. In ballet, the first one is called, logically enough, first position. It consists of standing with your heels together and your feet turned slightly outward. This is the basis for all other positions. Ballet dancers must learn it first in order to align their bodies so they will always be moving from their center of gravity. Other kinds of dancers, as well as golfers, football players, and virtually all types of professional athletes, do the same thing. They assume starting positions from which everything else flows.

The balanced or squared stance, your first position, must be your starting point for other important reasons. It focuses your audience's eyes where you want them, above the waist. If people are looking at your crossed feet and your twisted legs—the lower half of your torso—they will not see your upper half, and therefore you will not engage them with your eyes so that you can maintain eye contact with them. And eye contact is very important, as you'll see a bit later. Also, by making the correct lower body alignment, you properly align your upper body as well, making it all but impossible for your audience's focus to shift.

Sometimes when we make adjustments in the way we stand (or even sit), the new position doesn't feel right to us initially. In fact, it may feel wrong. It seems awkward, because though we were previously out of alignment and off kilter, to us that felt right.

I remember when I was learning to play tennis, I gripped the racket the way it felt good to me, with my wrist turned outward on the handle. In this way, when I raised my arm into position to hit the ball, the movement felt natural. A very nice gentleman came over to me one day, however, and suggested that I make an adjustment in my grip or I would seldom hit the ball, he said. He advised me to hold the racket straight out in front of me, so that I was in alignment with it, and to grip the handle with my wrist turned slightly to the left, as if I were shaking hands. "Now hold this position every time you raise your arm, and you will be in perfect position to hit the ball," he said.

I followed his advice and made the adjustment, but it felt wrong to me. In fact, it felt very awkward. But as I struggled to adjust to it, I saw that my shots were steadily getting better and that my ball was going over the net a lot more frequently than ever before. He was correct. Although the adjustment I'd made initially felt strange to me, it turned out to be absolutely right.

The same is true of public speaking and communicating. Each time you make an adjustment, however slight, you are improving your presentation presence incrementally. So, be aware that although the adjustment may not feel right to you at first, it will ultimately put you in the best position to communicate more naturally and effectively.

How to Move

Another reason why first position (a balanced stance) is important is that it facilitates movement. And you may *need* to move. All that energy pumping through your body may demand that you move to release some of it. But you must be able to control that movement so that it appears natural. This is what a balanced stance enables you to do quite easily.

Bill Clinton, one of the best speakers of our time, is great at controlling movement when he speaks; it always appears natural. He does this by starting off with a balanced stance and reassuming it after every move. You may recall Clinton's 1992 campaign against the first President Bush, in which he favored the so-called town meeting format for the presidential debates. There was a reason. This format allowed Clinton to move about freely so that he could get close to his audience and look into each member's eyes. He did this by starting from a balanced position. He would then take a few steps, either right or left, stop, and assume first position again. Then he would take a few more steps, perhaps closer to the audience this time, and stop once more to center himself again. He did this throughout the debate whenever it was his turn to talk. As a result, his movements looked completely natural.

If Clinton was nervous during his 1992 televised debates, it never showed. I remember watching him and thinking, "He makes it look so easy." That's because by starting from a balanced position, moving, then recentering himself each time, he was continually able to ground himself and control his flow of energy. This had the effect of keeping his audience grounded, as well, so that they focused on his message, not his movements.

Do's and Don'ts

Standing

DO

- Find your first position. Ground yourself—feet square and shoulder-width apart.
- Avoid getting tangled when moving, by always leading with the foot closer to the direction you are going. If you want to move right, lead with the right leg. If you are moving to the left, lead with the left leg.
- Resume first position and ground yourself each time you stop

Standing

DON'T
- Block energy and restrict movement by crossing feet or legs, leaning on or favoring one leg over the other or turning on your ankle
- Use repetitive movements evoking the cha-cha, salsa, or electric slide

Seated

DO
- Sit slightly forward on the chair, feet square on the floor, so that if someone theoretically were to pull the chair out from under you, you wouldn't automatically tip over or fall backward

DON'T
- Swivel or turn in the chair
- Be a slouch potato
- Slump or slide down in your seat (as if you were in a movie theater)

Physical Skill #2:   Breath Control

To Breathe or Not to Breathe

Question: "What happens when you don't breathe?"

Answer: "You die!"

It's as simple as that.

What happens when we get nervous as speakers is that (without even knowing it) we restrict our breathing capacity, which

Taking It up a Notch

It takes a lot of physical energy to get a message through to an audience. Avoid barriers that force you to use more energy than you would otherwise need. A podium, or lectern, can be such a barrier. If you ever find yourself in a situation in which you will be speaking or presenting from one, stand at least a foot back from it most of the time. This will give you ample room to gesture and release your physical energy (and not be perceived by your audience as hiding). And yes, it's okay to rest your hands lightly on the lectern from time to time as you speak. Just don't hold on to it with a death grip throughout your entire presentation. It's intended to support your notes, not you!

impacts our ability to communicate effectively. Our chests tighten, our throats close, our breathing becomes shallow or, in some cases, turns to gasps, all of which indicate that we are not taking in enough air. Improper breathing reduces the amount of air supply that enables us to control the length of our sentences and limits the options that add variety and interest to our communications. Learning proper breathing technique not only improves the sound of our voice and protects the overall health of our vocal instrument but has the added benefit of relieving much of the nervous tension we experience in stressful public speaking situations.

Proper Breathing Releases Tension

You may recall the movie *Broadcast News*, in which Holly Hunter plays an overachieving producer of a network news broadcast who is wound tighter than a drum. As she has risen to the top of her career, the pressures on her have become enormous. She deals with that pressure in a number of ways. One of them is releasing it emotionally through an extreme method that also provides comic relief for the moviegoer.

As her tension mounts on the morning of what is to be a particularly rough day, she sits on the edge of her bed, staring blankly into space, perfectly still, then, suddenly and unexpectedly, bursts into tears—not just quiet little sobs but loud wails that escalate in volume and intensity. Then, as quickly as the crying jag came on, it stops. She wipes her eyes, gets up, and goes about her business, completely fine.

This was the character's method of releasing tension. She literally sobbed it out of her system!

I'm not suggesting that you sit on the edge of the bed and sob before a presentation—though there is certainly no shame in shedding a few tears (and since you will be doing it in the privacy of your own home or office, who cares!). What I am suggesting is that breathing techniques can help you discharge tension, and, once it's discharged, all the energy bottled up behind it is free to work to your advantage.

Who knows what causes these reactions? Sometimes we're fine; other times, the pressure of a particular interview or speech is so intense we experience a more heightened degree of emotional or physical tension. The only thing that matters is having tools at your disposal to help you get back on track. If you feel out of control and can't think clearly, learn some simple breathing techniques. They work wonders.

Proper Breathing Calms You Down and Makes You Smart

As your breathing releases tension and you grow steadily calmer, you will find yourself more in tune with what is going on around you—you are "in the moment," as it is referred to in acting classes. In other words, you will no longer be focusing on the past (the tension and what caused it) but on the present. And being in the here and now makes us think more clearly.

In effect, what you are doing is allowing your frozen brain to thaw, thereby gaining access to your whole self again so that you can respond as you normally would. This allows you to be more spontaneous as you work on connecting with your audience.

Proper Breathing Supports Your Vocal Instrument

When clients tell me they get out of breath giving a speech or presentation, I know immediately that they are breathing improperly—they are interrupting the flow of air and weakening their vocal instrument.

Proper breathing not only removes the restricting tension, transforming it into energy, it also gives your vocal apparatus the support it needs to sustain itself.

How can you tell if you are breathing improperly? Here's a simple test: put your hands on your waist, then breathe in and out. If you notice that your chest is rising and falling as you breathe, you are breathing incorrectly. What you want to feel instead is your abdomen expanding and contracting as you breathe. If your waist is getting fatter, you are breathing correctly from the diaphragm. (However, don't be fooled into thinking you are putting on weight; diaphragmatic breathing actually tightens your tummy muscle!)

It is important to breathe from the diaphragm rather than from the chest, because this is how you increase the amount of air you are able to take in and release. When you breathe from the chest, you have limited access to the amount of breath you need to sustain your words. A great way to practice this skill is to lie on the floor on your back. Place a book on your abdomen. Inhale and exhale regularly so that the book goes steadily up and down. In this position, you will be forcing yourself to breathe from your diaphragm.

One of my acting teachers had me do this while reciting whole monologues from various plays. This exercise allowed me to train myself over time to build up and sustain the number of words I could speak without having to speed-talk or running out of breath. You can practice this exercise at home. It teaches you to perform diaphragmatic breathing as you speak aloud without having to think about it.

My Breathing Ritual

Knowing how and when to breathe serves you well in clearing your mind and body through all phases of the speechmaking process, from days or hours before the event, to just before you get up to speak, to all the way through to the end. I have a breathing ritual I go through at different stages before and during every public speaking engagement, as a way of relaxing myself and calming my internal chatter so that I am able to focus like a laser beam on the specific task at hand. Let me share it with you:

BEFORE THE EVENT
- Find a private place with no distractions (turn off cell phones, TVs, and radios) and sit quietly.
- Inhale five times and exhale five times, counting to yourself to focus your breathing.
- Take note of any emotional or physical tension, and breathe into the feeling or sensation.
- Repeat the sequence until you feel you have released it.

JUST BEFORE SPEAKING
- Inhale slowly and exhale slowly while setting your first position (standing or seated).
- Make eye contact, and inhale and exhale again, drawing the audience's focus toward you.
- When *you* are ready, begin to speak.

THROUGHOUT YOUR SPEECH
- Periodically check to see how you are breathing.

- If you notice you are speaking too quickly or are having trouble catching your breath, stop talking and pause.
- Inhale and exhale again slowly, breathing from your diaphragm. This will bring you back to your natural rhythm.
- Start speaking again, now that you're calm and back on track.

I once coached a gentleman who got very tense before making presentations. He said, "Ivy, I've tried everything! I run a couple of miles, I shadowbox, and nothing settles me down. I am generally a very controlled individual and can handle myself in any business setting. I don't know what to do!"

I recommended that he use my breathing ritual to help alleviate his anxiety, and I agreed to meet with him the morning he was about to give a very important presentation at an executive meeting, to go through the ritual with him.

I could tell he was uncomfortable because this normally outgoing, gregarious person was visibly withdrawn. We sat down and I showed him how to still his mind and focus on his breathing. As he breathed slowly, he started to feel resistance and described tightness in his chest. I asked him to simply breathe into that spot. He did as I asked and started to breathe very rapidly, but I told him not to worry. Within a few minutes the discomfort passed; his breathing slowed down and became even again.

When he finished he said he felt focused and energized. The tension had dissipated. He

FEARBUSTER

Don't panic if you have suddenly developed a cold on the eve of the event and can't breathe! Here's a trick I learned working in the theater when I often had to go on with the show after having come down with the sniffles. To help clear my sinuses, I would boil a pot of water (sometimes adding a drop of eucalyptus oil to it), bend over the pot with a towel over my head, and breathe in the steam. It loosened my chest congestion and often got me through—like magic!

learned that he didn't even have to know what the source of his tension was. All he had to do was take the time to quiet his mind and focus on breathing, to release the disturbance, and he could have access to his natural energy again.

Physical Skill #3: Eye Contact

Adds to Your Credibility

In normal one-on-one conversation, if the person you are speaking to averts his or her eyes or looks to the side of you, does that person instill in you a feeling of honesty and trust? Most likely your answer is no.

Being able to look someone straight in the eye so that you appear to be speaking directly to that person enhances what is arguably your most important asset in public speaking—your credibility.

This is important because one of the problems that arises when we get nervous in a public speaking situation is that we tend to avoid looking at our audience. We may glance at our listeners for a fleeting moment, or pretend we are looking as we gaze at some spot in the distance. The reason for this is that we are afraid to look them in the eye for fear of what we might see—namely, a blank expression or other nonverbal signals that we interpret negatively and take personally, even though very often what we are taking personally has nothing at all to do with us.

For example, I recall an occasion early on in my professional speaking career in which a man in the audience, sitting at the back of the room, looked completely miserable. Because I had some ambient anxiety as a beginner, I immediately concluded that I was responsible for his misery. At the break, he strolled my way and I thought: "Here's where he lets me have it." Instead he took my hand and shook it and told me how much he was enjoying my presentation. "I just wish I didn't have this pain," he said. "I had a root canal early this morning, and the Novocain has worn off."

Another time, I was speaking to a group of female business

executives and noticed that one of the women never smiled. The thought crossed my mind that she might be bored, so I made some on-the-spot adjustments to liven up my presentation a bit more, but this had no effect on her. I figured she was just not interested in what I had to say. At the end of my presentation, however, one of her associates pulled me aside and said, "I'm so glad Cindy was able to come and hear you today. She needed it. You see, her mother died recently, and this is her first day back."

Always keep this in mind: most likely *it's not about you. It's about them.*

The people who come to your speech or presentation or conduct your interview are bringing with them their life history and have many of its details fresh on their mind, just as you have. However, while you leave yours at the door to focus on the job at hand, they often carry theirs into the room with them. So, part of your job is to get them to let go of their lives and problems for a while and focus on your message. Looking them in the eye and establishing a direct line of communication with them serves to do that. It pulls them into the here and now and makes them more receptive to the experience of receiving your message.

Furthermore, by establishing eye contact with the person or persons you are speaking to, you get the on-the-spot feedback you need to be more effective. For example, you will pick up on whether your audience can hear you; can see your visuals or props, if you use them; looks confused by a point you've made that might require some quick clarifica-

FEARBUSTER

By shifting your focus off yourself and onto your audience, you become "other conscious." You become involved in the communication and your audience's concerns and let go of, or no longer notice, whatever initial anxiety you brought with you. Your audience also perceives you as a speaker who is sensitive to its needs!

tion; appears uncom-
fortable and distracted
because the room tem-
perature is getting too
hot or too cold; or is
growing restless—an
indicator, perhaps, that
you should pick up your
pace or cut some ma-
terial.

In effect, your listen-
ers are communicating
with you in a nonverbal
way. They are sending

FEARBUSTER

If you focus on making a connection with one person
at a time throughout your speech or presentation,
you will become less daunted at the prospect of
having to speak to a large group and less inclined
to feel overwhelmed by numbers. Instead, you
will feel as if you are having a one-on-one
conversation with certain individuals who
collectively make up that group.

you valuable cues, and only by maintaining eye contact can you
make use of that invaluable feedback to enhance your credibility
and increase your effectiveness.

Adds to Your Naturalness

Using eye contact effectively can help you affect a more natural, conversational style of delivery, engaging your audience in a
dialogue, or conversation, between you and them. A one-sided
conversation makes the recipient feel that he or she is being talked
at, not with—that you are basically conversing with yourself, that
you don't care what kind of a response you get because you are
going to say what you are going to say no matter what. This creates a breach between you and your listener, a breach that says
one of you isn't needed, and so your listener's attention figuratively takes its leave.

Adds to Your Energy Level

All audiences are different. If you look at and listen to them
carefully, the nonverbal signals you pick up will show you how to
shift your energy level accordingly.

Do's and Don'ts

DO

- Look at individuals
- Converse one on one
- Talk through a thought or point with one person, then move to the next
- Take in all areas of the room
- Have the lights turned up if you can't see all the faces
- Come down off the stage or move in closer, if necessary, to make eye contact

DON'T

- Focus on one place (e.g., the back wall)
- Get into a staring contest with anyone
- Make anyone feel uncomfortable by focusing on them too long
- Dart your eyes back and forth
- Picture your audience naked (as we've often been told): you may laugh, cry, or run from the room!

For example, in large auditoriums especially, you can actually feel an exchange of energy with the audience. It is a force and experiencing it can be fun. On occasions when you feel tired, sick, or otherwise not up to the task of speaking to a large group, this exchange can give you just the boost you need to elevate your own energy level to match the audience's.

Don't get me wrong. There are times when all the energy seems to be flowing one way, from you. This just means you will have to work harder to engage the audience and boost its energy level. Sustained eye contact is a surefire way of doing this.

Start by looking at one person in that sea of faces, and when you feel that you are connecting with that person, that an honest exchange of energy is occurring between the two of you, move on to the next person and make eye contact until the same exchange of energy occurs. And you will be on your way!

Putting It All Together

I coached a man recently who was technically a very effective speaker. He had a resonant voice and spoke with ease, his thoughts were well organized and fluidly expressed, and he was confident in his knowledge of his topic. Sounds great, right? Not exactly. He had one significant problem standing in his way. His audience thought he was patronizing.

He made no attempt to connect with his listeners. In fact, he wouldn't look at them. He walked about the stage and only occasionally glanced their way but never made sustained eye contact. The result was that he came across as if he were talking down to them, which did not make for a very good impression.

I suggested that to solve this problem he should try making eye contact with every member of the audience as he spoke, and to do it this way:

Look at one person in the audience, complete a thought, then shift eye contact to another person to make the next point, then move on to the next person to share the next thought, and so on, reaching as many people as he could, in no particular order, until he was finished. Great communicators make you feel as if they are talking to you and to you alone, I told him. And eye contact is how you do it.

He did as I suggested. Initially he seemed uncomfortable (later he told me it made him feel shy and vulnerable), but as he continued he got more relaxed and began smiling at the audience, his delivery got more conversational, more natural, and the audience took to him. What a difference this very small change had made in the way he was presenting himself physically. He became more

likable and approachable. It resulted in his listeners' feeling they
were now part of the conversation—that they mattered.

Physical Skill #4:   Hand Placement and Gestures

"What do I do with my hands?"

I am amazed by how many people ask me this question. When
I ask why, they tell me things like, "My college teacher said never
to move my hands when I speak—to always keep them at my side.
I'm Italian and that's really hard for me!"

Not to move your hands when you speak is a ridiculous instruction. If you naturally move your hands in casual conversation, it's
equally natural for you to move them in a public speaking situation.
And, after all, isn't tapping into your authentic self to achieve a delivery style that is natural what speaking without fear is all about?

The real issue is not whether to use your hands but, as with the
other physical skills I am discussing in this chapter, how to use
your hands. It's okay to do anything with your hands in a public
speaking situation—put your hands in your pockets, place them
on the podium, or wave them in the air—but not all the time.
Hand actions and gestures can help listeners better understand
your message. But moderation is key.

Easy as 1-2-3

When we get nervous speaking, we have a tendency to use our
hands in ways that distract the audience from hearing our message
and may even take us down a peg in the eyes of the audience by
fostering a very different image than the one we sought to project.

For example, a senior management executive I worked with
had a habit of wiggling her hands at her side when she got nervous speaking. She sported long, red lacquered nails, which
drew more attention to her hands. The movement was so distracting and disconcerting that she unwittingly projected an

Do's and Don'ts

DO

- Keep hands above the waist
- Find a resting position for your hands
- Make gestures clear and definite
- Vary movements
- Show as well as tell

DON'T

- Repeat the same gesture constantly
- Overuse hand movement, even if varied
- Keep hands in pockets. If you do plan to occasionally put your hand in your pocket, remember to remove the change. Jingling change is *very* distracting.
- Hang on to podiums or lecterns for dear life
- Use wild, uncontrolled movements or nondescript gestures

entry-level image, not a senior-level executive image that reflected her position.

With that in mind, here's an easy but effective way to remember what to do with your hands when speaking or communicating publicly, and deciding how much is too much:

1. Keep your hands above your waist. If you start with your hands below your waist and you are battling nerves, it becomes very hard to raise them even an inch, because when we get nervous we tend to inhibit our movements. So, keeping your hands above your waist gives them a shorter dis-

tance to climb and move freely. (Of course it's okay to occasionally rest them at your sides, but make sure to get them back up again to access your natural style.)

2. Just as with your feet, decide upon a comfortable first position to rest your hands in between movements—for example, lightly clasping one hand over the other, cupping them together with the fingertips touching, and occasionally letting them fall to your sides. I have seen each of these methods used quite effectively.

3. Let your hands do what comes naturally to you as you talk, but vary their movements. For example, don't stick with one gesture, like wagging your finger, and repeat it over and over. Live by these words of Ron Arden, one of the most respected professional speakers and coaches in the business: "The enemy of the speaker is sameness."

Physical Skill #5:   Vocal Power

Add Some PEP to Your Vocal Instrument

Imagine getting up to speak and, despite your having honed your physical skills in the four previous areas, your voice starts to shake, and you emit an almost inaudible sound that you barely recognize as your own voice. And you continue speaking in that tiny monotone, eventually putting your listeners to sleep.

This is one of the most common symptoms of repressed nervous energy, one that not only affects the way we sound but has the greatest effect on how we come across to our audience. The disheartening look of confusion we see on the faces of our listeners if they can't hear or understand us just drives us further inward, and all systems start shutting down.

This is why it's imperative to work on this last physical skill. Having prepared a great speech or presentation, and fine-tuned your body movements and delivery style, you don't want to ruin it all by not being heard.

Here are some effective solutions for avoiding the situation I just described (or turning it around quickly) by adding some PEP — Projection, Enunciation, and Pace — to your vocal instrument.

Projection

Voice projection is a key ingredient in releasing repressed nervous energy and relieving your tension immediately. It works not only to free your voice so you can be heard, it also releases some of your pent-up nervous energy. All you have to do is make a conscious effort to pump up the volume to a point where you feel comfortable and you see your audience is staying involved because it hears you.

You don't need voice or speech lessons or the voice of a professional anchorperson or actor to project. You just have to remember that your listeners need to hear you, decide on the volume level that will achieve this in the particular environment, and then work to sustain that volume.

In large rooms especially, unless you are wearing a microphone, it will be necessary to project your voice in order to be heard by everyone. The easiest way to do this is to pick a person in the audience who is farthest away from you and start by speaking to that person. Adjust your volume so that person can hear you, and sustain that level as you move around the room. You can even use the same technique in a conference room setting where you are sitting down. You may think because you are sitting down, you can speak in a conversational tone and not quite as much voice projection is required. However, if you are nervous, just as with standing on your feet, your tendency will be to speak too softly. The same rule applies here. Pick out the person who is seated farthest away from you at the conference table, and start by speaking to that person. In either situation, you get a double advantage from projecting your voice; as you must physically exert yourself to up your volume to any level, you automatically release any nervous tension you may be feeling, and make yourself relax.

Many people I coach in workshops think at first that even the slightest adjustment in their volume makes them come across like they are shouting. But when I ask the others in the workshop to be the judge, 99 percent of the time their reaction is that the speaker still isn't loud enough, let alone shouting or overbearing.

Other people I work with don't project because they don't like the sound of their own voice for some reason. For example, Anne is a formidable business professional who is highly respected throughout her company. She is superb at analyzing business issues, formulating effective strategies to address them, and managing people. But in a public speaking situation, she speaks very very softly—so softly, in fact, that she projects an image of timidity rather than confidence and authority.

As we worked on increasing her vocal projection, she became increasingly uncomfortable. Finally, she let the cat out of the bag. She said that when she projected her voice at the level I suggested was sufficient for this particular room, it reminded her of her mother, who always sounded negative and critical and spoke loudly. It wasn't that she didn't have the ability to project her voice. It was that she wanted to avoid sounding like her mother at all costs—even at the risk of undermining her professional image.

I reminded Anne that no one, including me, knew what her mother sounded like, so no comparison could be made, except by her. It was essential for her to make the effort to be heard, if only not to tarnish her image. Once she realized what the underlying issue was behind her sotto voce, she was able to be more objective. With practice and positive feedback from me and others in the workshop, she was soon able to project her voice quite well in spite of the negative association she had with doing so. This solution may not have addressed the underlying issue of why she disliked the sound of her projected voice, but it effectively addressed the more urgent issue of not being heard, which is what mattered most immediately.

Enunciation

It is not enough that your listeners hear you; they must *under-stand* you as well. So often, when we project our voices, we slip into the same old bad habits we have in casual conversation — namely, we drop consonants and slur or swallow our words. Perhaps this is because in our information age, much of our daily communication is no longer done face-to-face but electronically, through faxes, e-mails, and instant messaging. We have become rusty in the art of enunciation (assuming we ever learned or practiced it to begin with).

Making yourself understood in a public speaking situation demands practice, especially if you have a pronounced regional, ethnic, or foreign accent. To do this, I recommend you practice by reading out loud. As you go about your daily routine, find opportunities to get used to shaping words with your lips and tongue so they emerge more clearly and fully. When you have to read something — a memorandum, e-mail message, magazine article, or whatever — *read it aloud*. You can do this in the privacy of your own home or office so you won't feel foolish.

If you have kids or nieces and nephews, reading stories to them out loud will give you excellent practice enunciating — especially Dr. Seuss stories, which have many challenging tongue twisters in them. This kind of exercise can be great fun. And by doing it just a few minutes each day, you will make great strides quickly in your ability to enunciate.

Pace

The last mistake — and arguably the most common one — people make when communicating in a public forum (particularly if they are nervous) is speaking either too fast or too slowly.

Speaking too quickly makes you come across as if you can't wait for the whole ordeal to be over, which is not the best way to win over your audience. So, slow down and take an occasional pause (if only to fill your lungs with air, which is always a good idea). But don't slow down and pause too much or you may come across to your audience as stilted and stuffy—like Al Gore.

"Okay, Ivy," you say, "I've got the idea: slow down, but not too much or too little, and pause once in a while. But what constitutes 'too much,' 'too little,' and 'a while'? Is there a rule of thumb?"

Not really. It's not like a typing course that gives you an average of so many words a minute to shoot for, or running the marathon, for which you train yourself to take an average of so many breaths a minute in order to reach the finish line without collapsing. As I've emphasized throughout this book, in public speaking, it's doing what comes naturally that always works best.

To achieve *your* right pace, you must first get used to hearing the sound of your voice. Initially, this may seem like a ridiculous statement ("Of course I know the sound of my voice! I've been living with it for years!"), but the fact is we tend to have a very different perception of how we sound, of how quickly or slowly we speak, than others do.

So, here's what to do to get over that hump and find your own pace. Take out your CD or audiocassette recorder and read a magazine article into it. Experiment with inflections. Then play back the audio and listen, *really listen*. Familiarize yourself with the rhythms of your own voice, its natural speed and natural intervals between breaths. Then repeat the exercise, making adjustments accordingly until the voice you hear back is the voice you had always *thought* you'd heard—the one whose projection, enunciation and pace, and overall personality is most naturally *you*.

Seeing Is Believing

It is important to assess your physical skills when you start and then as you progress in order to make needed adjustments. One way of doing this is to ask a friend or family member to sit in on your practice sessions and offer feedback. But if you go that route, be sure to choose someone who can be supportive. By supportive, I don't mean someone who is so worried about hurting your feelings that he or she will tell you only how wonderful you are. You want someone who is eager to see you succeed, but who can be objective in his or her opinion, and is willing to share that opinion with you.

At the opposite extreme, you don't want someone who focuses only on what you are doing "wrong," either. I've heard from clients about public speaking instructors whose methodology was to accentuate the negative and eliminate the positive. That's not being objective, either, and is counterintuitive to one of the primary goals of coaching and practicing public speaking, which is to build the speaker's self-confidence. If all the speaker ever hears about is what he or she is doing badly, the person will likely not progress very far.

A second way to go is to assess your own progress. This is the best route, because in my experience we are our own toughest critics. So, here's a suggestion: videotape yourself.

The video camera is an invaluable tool for gauging your before-and-after performance and achieving ongoing improvement, because seeing truly is believing. Of course, seeing can also be a bit disconcerting—at least initially; in some sense, we are all at least a little camera shy (except, perhaps, Madonna). I know the first time I saw myself on tape, I had to leave the room. But I got used to it and have used the video camera in my workshops and for my own improvement ever since.

Put the video camera on a tripod, and use the remote control to record yourself if you insist on complete privacy, or rope in that supportive friend or family member to push the Record button for you and to pan the camera if necessary to keep you in the frame when you are practicing moving around.

As with recording yourself on CD or audiotape, you can conveniently video your practice sessions in your home or at your office. Start out by giving a mock speech or presentation, or participating in a mock interview. (To keep the practice session as close to reality as possible, ask a friend to be the interviewer, so that you will not be talking to yourself.) Initially and as you monitor your progress, you will find moments when you think you come across worse than you actually do, and other moments when you think you are coming across better than you really are.

For example, I worked with a client who insists she is a positive person, yet the feedback she gets from her colleagues after every presentation is to the contrary. She was able to obtain a videotape of a recent presentation she'd given, and we watched it together. This was the first time she had ever seen herself as others did in a "performance situation," and as she watched, I noticed she started fidgeting and an unhappy expression washed over her face.

I asked her to start by telling me what she liked about herself on the tape. She said she couldn't come up with anything. I reminded her that her content was strong and well organized, and I highlighted other positive attributes she possessed; then I asked her what she saw that made her feel so uncomfortable.

"That I never smile," she answered. "And all along I thought I did." She called her posture sloppy, and observed that she had a stern and overbearing look that was not at all how she had perceived herself, and certainly not the way she wanted to come across to her colleagues. "Wow, do I have to make some changes!" she said.

The video camera is an excellent tool for doing this on your own.

Here are some pointers for identifying your strengths and weaknesses before, and monitoring your progress after:

Guidelines for Assessing Your Physical Skills

▌ Focus separately on each of the five physical skills — balance, breath control, eye contact, hand placement and gestures, vocal power.

▌ Start by assessing the positive side of the equation in each area. Find a couple of things you like about what you see — things you do that make you come across naturally and authentically. This creates a benchmark against which to determine what is unnatural, inauthentic, or distracting, and why.

▌ Don't be too defensive or too hard on yourself. You don't have to be a Tony Robbins or look like a movie star! The objective is to get an accurate assessment of what is going on in each skill area so that you can put together a plan for dealing successfully with the changes that you need to make.

▌ Give yourself all the ammunition you need to get your delivery style to the next level. As you isolate each skill area, ask yourself the following questions about what you see, and answer why "yes" or why "no."

1. "Do I come across naturally and confidently?"

2. "Do I recognize the person I see?" (For example, you may think of yourself as outgoing and expressive, but the person you see is low-key and practically inaudible.)

3. "Does my behavior match my words?" (For example, you are saying, "I am very happy to be here today," but everything else about you speaks, "Help, I'm being held prisoner!")

4. "If the person I am watching were not me, would I *believe* that person?"

5. "If the person I am watching were not me, would that person hold my attention for more than a minute?"

6. "Is that behavior distracting?" (For example, you move around so much that you look like a duck in a shooting gallery. The behavior needs addressing, because if it is distracting to you, it probably will be to your listeners, as well, and will take their focus off your message.)

▌ Hang on to the tape(s)! Don't record your next practice sessions or this month's episodes of your favorite TV show over them—at least not yet. You will need them, both as a record of what must still be worked on and as positive reinforcement of how far you have come.

▌ Choose one or two skills to work on at a time. You may find that as you are working on vocal projection, your gestures and overall energy automatically improve.

▌ Keep track of how you feel about, and how others are responding to, your new delivery style.

▌ Take your time. We're not talking life or death here (or even snakes)! What initially seemed so difficult and daunting will eventually become so easy and enjoyable it will surprise you.

Ordinary People—Extraordinary Impact

Have you ever had the experience of listening to a speaker and suddenly finding yourself processing the words on a deeper, more meaningful level that makes you nod in recognition and understanding?

There are many different reasons why this phenomenon occurs. It may happen because of the nature of the subject itself and your interest in it. It may happen because of the speaker's skill in putting ideas together and shaping the content of his or her message. Or it may be because of the speaker's manner and physical presence; from the way the speaker uses his or her body language and vocal instrument, you get a sense that you are seeing and hearing the real person, not a persona the speaker has slipped on for the occasion. You get the feeling the speaker is comfortable in his or her own skin—is honestly conveying the essence of who he or she is. In other words, the person is authentic. These elements are what make us tune in to the speaker's words so deeply.

I can recall a particular speaker I found riveting. He was

addressing a group of businesspeople at a technology conference and had all of us in the audience mesmerized. He simply stood center stage on a large platform and told a story of survival in a World War II concentration camp. He spoke simply, only occasionally moving about the stage, but for most of his speech he stood still. Throughout, I felt as though he was speaking directly to me.

On another occasion, I watched a speaker who dashed out onstage in a rush of energy. He bolted downstage to one side, looked at someone at random in the front row, and hurled an unexpected question at the person, causing the audience to burst out laughing at the person's reaction. The speaker then darted over to the other side of the stage and hurled another question at another randomly selected member of the audience. Again, we responded with laughter. Then he proceeded to launch into his speech, which he delivered in a crisp forty-five minutes — during which all of us in the audience found ourselves laughing as much as hanging on his every word, wondering what he would say or do next. His energy was infectious. He was tremendously physical in his presentation style; he shook his fists in the air, pounded on a prop table, even sprawled onstage on one occasion to demonstrate a point he wanted to make. But he was so skilled in the use of his energy and his body that at no time did his exuberance overwhelm us or get in the way of his message. He knew exactly how to go about creating the effect he desired.

When I met him afterward, I spotted right away that even though his offstage persona was considerably lower key than what I had witnessed onstage, he was nevertheless the same person — animated and humorous, just a little less so. He was able to take these aspects of himself and heighten them onstage.

Though the delivery style of these two speakers was vastly different, both styles were equally effective — because the style was authentic. These speakers were being true to themselves, and they came across that way.

This is what you are striving to achieve. When you employ the five physical skills laid out in this chapter, you have the foundation you need to redirect your energy and achieve an animated and engaging delivery style that is authentic to yourself. In other words, a delivery style that speaks to your audience in a manner that communicates the real you. This is where your real strength lies.

8

You Can't Dance Until
You Know the Steps:
the Power of Rehearsal

Tips and Techniques for Rehearsing

In the theater, rehearsal is an integral part of the performance process. You rehearse to learn your lines and discover the character you are playing; then, when you step onstage, the magic of having an audience takes over and, if you are well prepared, you have an opportunity to experience the joy of creating a partnership among you, the character you play, and your audience.

As I shifted careers and started my work helping businesspeople and others to speak without fear, I came to the realization that knowing how to rehearse, when to rehearse, and the rehearsal options are just as important to creating a successful speech, presentation, or having a successful interview as they are in the theater.

Rehearsal is the final piece of the puzzle. It is the piece that not only gives you the final boost of confidence you need to be able to communicate powerfully, but also the piece that frees you to be spontaneous and fully present so that you can *enjoy* public speaking. It is the gateway to unleashing your natural style of delivery and being your authentic self.

There are three types of rehearsal:

1. The verbal rehearsal
2. The physical/technical rehearsal
3. The mental rehearsal

Depending upon your nervousness profile, you may need to spend more time on one type than another. For example, Improvisers, who typically underrehearse or leave everything to chance but are creative, intuitive, and innately self-confident, will likely need to spend more time on the verbal and the physical/technical rehearsal so as not to veer off course from their message and confuse their audience, whereas the more extreme profiles like Avoiders will need as much of all three types of rehearsal as they can manage. For everyone, however, a *minimum amount* of rehearsal in all three areas will always be necessary to achieve a successful outcome in any public speaking situation, because, quite frankly, practice makes for a compelling, confident presentation. Whether you are an Avoider, an Anticipator, an Adrenalizer, or an Improviser, once you develop your own ritual for rehearsal, it will become as second nature to you as breathing—an integral part of your way of working.

The Verbal Rehearsal

Rehearse Aloud

Whether you are giving a speech or presentation or are preparing for an interview, rehearse *out loud*.

Many people believe that if they silently go over the text of their speech, the outline of their presentation, or the notes they've put together for their interview, this will suffice. But the problem with rehearsing in your head is that you always sound great. The words are carefully chosen and articulated correctly, the flow of the material is smooth, and your "performance" is always on the money. However, when the time comes and you actually begin to speak, your bubble bursts. Your ideas may come across as unclear or directionless. You may come across as less sure of yourself as you start stumbling over words and filling in gaps with distracting "um's" and "er's." The result? On-the-spot anxiety.

On the other hand, by speaking aloud the actual words or ideas you will be communicating, you get a feel for how those words will sound and how the material will flow at the event itself. Upon hearing them, you may realize that you don't want to express an idea a particular way, and be able to come up with an alternative that is clearer and more persuasive. In fact, you may come up with a number of alternatives that present opportunities for improving the presentation overall—improvements that will lead to a bigger, better payoff with your audience.

Edit as You Go

Editing your material to refine your message is an ongoing process. As you rehearse aloud, you may discover there is still too much information and decide to further limit your message (or, perhaps, change it entirely). And when you're on your feet in the physical/technical rehearsal, you may find that even more editing is necessary.

In most speaking situations, working from notes or an outline with bullets is sufficient and will facilitate the editing process. However, in high-stakes speaking situations (especially if you are an Improviser), I recommend at first writing out every bit of information you will be covering so that you will have something more substantial to edit from; you then reduce it to notes or bullets and make any other changes you may wish as you move through the other types of rehearsal.

To Memorize or Not to Memorize

In the theater, you must memorize everything about your character and performance, from your lines to your stage movements, for a number of reasons. Because your dialogue contributes to moving the play along, you must know it cold and speak it exactly as written (an actor will get fired sometimes for having altered the playwright's words even just slightly). Often, your words are to cue another actor onstage. Let's say one of your lines is "Hail, Caesar! Caesar cometh!" If you haven't got it down and don't say it, Caesar might not cometh!

Public speaking is a different type of performance situation. Here, familiarization, not memorization, is the key. You want to avoid coming across as stiff and unnatural or, as it is referred to in my business, as a "talking head." Committing every word, phrase, idea, or concept to memory may cause that to happen.

My client Cindy, a wonderful informal communicator, is a good example of this. Her style is loose, she's passionate, and her impact is powerful. But when it comes to giving a formal presentation or a speech, she turns into a different person. Worried that she may forget a point, she plots out and memorizes every single note or word, losing her personality in the process along with the very charisma and energy that would make her message unique and her presentation memorable.

When you are preparing for a public speaking situation, the repetitive nature of the rehearsal process enables you to remember *what* you must say and know *why* you are saying it so you can relax enough onstage to deliver it confidently. If you are an Anticipator like Cindy who feels the need to memorize *something* in order to feel secure, my recommendation is to memorize your opening, your close, and your transitions. This will give you the security you are looking for without losing the style that makes the substance of your message sing.

If you are interviewing for a job or college or pitching a client, you especially want to familiarize yourself thoroughly with your key ideas rather than memorize a prepared script word for word. The verbal rehearsal will help you achieve that. In order to feel confident that I would not overlook or forget anything about each prospect, here's how I went about my verbal rehearsal preparing for a series of meetings in which I would be selling my services as a public speaking coach to some very important prospects. A lot was at stake. Each prospect was different, so there was much to be learned and remembered about each one so that I would know how to shape my message accordingly.

- I wrote my key questions about each prospect on a separate index card, along with my answers to these questions in bulleted form, so that what I needed in order to familiarize myself with each prospect would be at my fingertips.
- I carried these index cards around with me and would pull one out at random while riding in a cab, doing my grocery shopping, or doing some other fairly routine activity.
- I'd select a question on the prospect's card, read it to myself, and answer it out loud.

This constituted my verbal rehearsal, which I carried out at my convenience during the week leading up to the meetings until I was able to net out the essential information on each card and convey my targeted message cleanly and concisely. In this way, my message stayed always on track, though the words or gestures I used to convey that message would change slightly each time, thereby keeping each "perfor-

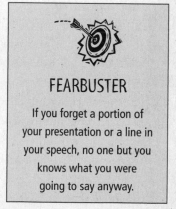

FEARBUSTER

If you forget a portion of your presentation or a line in your speech, no one but you knows what you were going to say anyway.

Taking It up a Notch

If you will be reading from a fully scripted speech, the more you rehearse to familiarize yourself with the text, the less you will find yourself looking down as you give the speech. Thus, you will maintain more eye contact with your audience, an important ingredient in connecting with your audience and driving your message home (see chapter 7).

mance" fresh. By the time each meeting rolled around, I was in great shape to be spontaneous. I could add or subtract ideas or go in a completely different direction if needed, yet always bring my interviewers back to where I wanted them to be.

The Physical/Technical Rehearsal

Do a Site Survey

One of the most overlooked safety nets that you can provide yourself with is performing what is known as a site survey. If possible, visit beforehand the location where you will be speaking, presenting, or lecturing so that you can see the environment you will be working in. This will allow you to compile firsthand a list of what you might need to bring with you (beyond the normal extras you should carry) that the location may not be able to provide (e.g., AC adapters for older buildings).

If it is not possible to do a site survey in person, call the venue ahead with a checklist of questions so that you can in effect conduct your site survey over the phone. If you are told there is an

AV technician who will be handling your speech, presentation, or lecture, ask to speak with that person. The AV technician can make you look and sound like a pro, so you really want to make him or her your ally.

For my seminars and workshops, I work with an audiovisual whiz named Rick Rothery, with whom I've been associated almost since I started in this business. Rick has been providing AV to many Fortune 500 companies as well as for live theatrical events since 1964, and I couldn't do without him. His advice is that even if you do a survey on-site or over the phone, you should still plan to arrive extra early the day of your event so that you can find out *what might have changed* since then, as well as learn things (there will always be some) that you may not have been told about.

Remember that Murphy's Law is always lurking in the background, waiting to strike. So, give yourself plenty of time to check out all the technical aspects of your speech, presentation, or lecture environment, such as computer equipment, lighting, video equipment, screens, lecterns, chairs, tables, and so on. This is especially critical if you are a one-person band and must manage the stage aspects of your performance situation yourself. But even with a strong AV technician as your ally, you should assume as much responsibility yourself for checking things out as you comfortably can—because *you* have the greatest vested interest in ensuring your success.

A client named Sheila was asked to speak at a financial association's conference for women. She had enthusiastically agreed but was now faced with a dilemma and needed my advice. She explained that she had requested some time prior to the event to rehearse on the stage along with the equipment the conference center was providing (as part of her preparation, she hoped to work out any potential snags in the visual part of her presentation). She was told, however, that because deadlines were tight, her request could not be accommodated.

"What should I do?" she asked me.

"Don't take no for an answer!" came my reply. I said that she should insist on that rehearsal time or tell them she would have to reconsider her commitment to appear. After all, while it might be *their* conference, it was *her* name and reputation on the line. Always take care of yourself first!

She did as I suggested and this time was given the on-site rehearsal time she requested. It made a big difference. When I spoke with her after the event, she said her speech was very well received. But without that rehearsal time on the floor, things might have gone quite another way, as behind her on the stage were large floor-to-ceiling video screens that projected images of her speaking. (She was referring to I-Mag, or image magnification screens, that are commonly used in conference settings.)

Being able to rehearse ahead of time in the actual space with the equipment she would be using helped her do some last-minute trimming of the number of slides she'd intended to use—thus making her presentation even tighter so that there were no "dead spots." As a result, she became more comfortable and her confidence increased.

Here's another story demonstrating the need for on-the-spot rehearsal time. This one, though, is about me.

I once had a speaking engagement at the McCormick Center in Chicago. The auditorium was quite sizable, and about 450 executives were expected to attend. I would need lighting and sound equipment in order to be properly seen and heard by such a large group. I scheduled a technical rehearsal for one o'clock the day before the conference. I arrived for my rehearsal on time and was met by a technician who informed me quite unexpectedly that "due to union regulations" there could be no technical rehearsal.

I controlled my anxiety as much as possible and explained that in order to acclimate myself I had to get the lights arranged and make sure the sound equipment worked. "Isn't there any time at all?" I asked.

"Sorry, ma'am," he said. "But the only time we might have available is four A.M."

After trying unsuccessfully to locate the people who hired me for the conference and get them to intervene on my behalf, I decided to get what I needed on my own, come hell or high water.

I went back into the auditorium, plopped myself into a seat, and told the technician that I absolutely, positively would not budge until I got my technical rehearsal time!

Seeing my determination, he decided finally to take pity on me (or maybe just wanted to get rid of me), and said, "Okay, I'll bend the 'union rules' and do this right now." I went onstage to go through my speech as he turned on the lights, which were set at a standard output, and what happened then was like the arrival of the mother ship in *Close Encounters of the Third Kind*. I was blinded! I could see nothing, absolutely nothing. Not the stage, not the auditorium, not even my script!

As my sight inched back, the technician made the necessary adjustments to the settings of the lights, and this time the technical rehearsal went off without a hitch. Afterward, I made my way back to my hotel to rest up for the main event the next day, relieved that I hadn't given in to those "union rules." Imagine what would have happened if I'd gone before those 450 executives without having insisted on the rehearsal time to protect myself (and thereby ensure a successful outcome). I definitely would have had a close encounter—of a very strange kind, indeed!

There will be occasions, of course, when you may not be able to rehearse on the spot ahead of time—for example, you're flying in from somewhere and get delayed, or you have to fill in for someone at the last minute. But these occasions are exceptions. The general rule is that in most situations and venues, there is *always* time available. So, take advantage of it. Get in the habit of asking for some time, however minimal, to do a physical/technical rehearsal in the environment where you will be speaking or presenting—with the actual equipment (if any) you will be using. And don't take No for an answer.

■ ■ ■

Even if you are rehearsing for an upcoming job interview, you can still do a form of physical rehearsing. You can replicate the general characteristics of the environment where you will probably be interviewed by setting up a desk and chair. Then you can role-play a mock interview by having a friend or family member throw questions at you. As suggested in chapter 7, videotape your "performance" to see how you come across in your answers and body language.

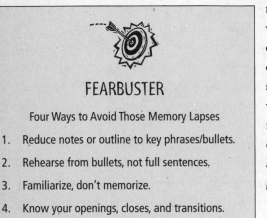

FEARBUSTER

Four Ways to Avoid Those Memory Lapses

1. Reduce notes or outline to key phrases/bullets.
2. Rehearse from bullets, not full sentences.
3. Familiarize, don't memorize.
4. Know your openings, closes, and transitions.

In every case, the act of physically rehearsing your speech, presentation, or interview is a great tool for putting your focus where it needs to be.

The Mental Rehearsal

I read an article once about Liu Chi Kung, the famous Chinese concert pianist who placed second to America's Van Cliburn in the celebrated 1958 international competition in which Cliburn became a star. Liu Chi Kung's career was going great guns when suddenly, for some reason, he ran afoul of his country's Communist government and was jailed as a political prisoner. He spent the next seven years of his life in confinement without being able to play a note.

Taking It up a Notch

Take an acting class or a course in improvisation to hone your verbal and physical rehearsal skills. Even though public speaking is not giving a performance in the same sense that an actor gives one, picking up some of the stage techniques actors use is not only a great way to improve your skills in these very important areas, but also a great way to break inhibitions.

After his release from prison, Liu Chi Kung rejoined the concert tour and was soon wowing the music critics with his ability to play the piano as if he'd never been away from the concert stage. In fact, most of the critics said he was playing even better than he had before!

How was it possible that Liu Chi Kung was able to come back so strongly without being able to practice a note for seven long years?

He says that he did practice, every single day in his cell, playing every note of every concert piece he'd ever played onstage over and over again in his mind!

This technique is called rehearsing mentally, and I use it myself prior to every speech, workshop, or business meeting as a way of visualizing how I want everything to go—so that my subconscious will get into the act and help make it happen.

The mental rehearsal spins off the visualizing exercise in chapter 5, which is part of the process of clearing away inhibitions. Adapted here as a method of rehearsing, its purpose is similar. By visualizing yourself giving that speech, making that presentation, or being interviewed for that job, you will engage your subconscious to help you turn what you are imagining into reality. For Avoiders and Anticipators particularly, it is an especially potent tool.

The basic premise is that thought precedes action. Our thoughts have considerable influence over us—and they can be tipped one way or the other by the power of suggestion. Oprah Winfrey demonstrated this on an episode of her syndicated talk show one afternoon when she conducted a test of the power of suggestion on her unsuspecting studio audience. When the audience arrived for the taping of the show, she told the members that a scent had been released into the studio and that she wanted to know by the end of the show if they had smelled it and could identify it. When the time came, many told her they had indeed smelled it—some even said the scent was all over their clothes!

But then Oprah broke the news. She had lied. No such scent had been emitted into the studio. The audience only thought there had been one because they had been influenced to think that way—and actually smelled a scent as a result!

This is the power of suggestion.

What the mental rehearsal does is use that power in a positive manner to fill our minds with positive thoughts and images of how successful we will be with our performance, thereby bringing that successful performance about. In other words, by practicing in our minds what is possible, we tap our honest desire to make it probable and spur that probability to become reality.

The mental rehearsal complements the verbal and physical/technical rehearsal by being the weight that finally tips the scale completely in our favor.

A Habit for Life

In my previous life, I once had to go on in place of the lead actress in an off-Broadway show. We were three weeks into the run of the show, and, as the understudy, I had not had a full rehearsal yet. So, imagine my shock when I arrived at the theater expecting to have to do nothing but watch and suddenly found that because of unforeseen circumstances, I would be going on that night in place of the star!

I had three hours to prepare! My heart started pounding. Fortunately, I had too much to do to think about how nervous I was. I was rushed into costume and makeup while reviewing my lines and lyrics simultaneously. As I and the other actors would be using live microphones with long cords, each of us had to know when and where to cross the stage so as to avoid a collision. These moves had been very carefully choreographed. My head was spinning trying to remember my character's moves from having watched them offstage.

What no one knew but me, however, was that I had left little to chance. In the event that a situation like this might occur, I had been rehearsing the part every night in my room after the show, on my own.

Showtime arrived. As I awaited my entrance backstage, I could hear the tide of voices washing through the auditorium as the audience filed in and people took their seats. The lights went down. I took a deep breath (several, in fact) and did a quick, last-minute mental rehearsal, visualizing my performance as I wanted it to be—and, in my mind's eye, pulling it off just that way. The curtain went up. I made my entrance. And took off on a wild adventure.

At the end of the show, I stood downstage and sang the final song. It was an emotional moment for the character, and I had tears streaming down my face. The audience must have thought I was one heck of an actress. The truth is, I wasn't crying because of the character's journey, I was crying because the show was ending and I hadn't accidentally killed anyone onstage!

It was an emotional and thrilling evening. I received a standing ovation, and all I could think to myself was . . . thank god I rehearsed.

Rehearsal time is a gift that you give to yourself. Get in the habit of taking it. Do as much verbal, physical/technical, and mental rehearsing as you need in order to feel fully confident about that next speech or presentation you have to make or that next interview you must go on. In other words, build in the minimum *you* need (which may change as you become more skillful), *and stick to it.*

You'll have an advantage for life!

9

Putting It All Together: It's Showtime!

You've Come a Long Way, Baby!

It is time at last to wrap things up by addressing the "stage management" issues involved in communicating effectively. These are the last-minute details to pay attention to the day of the event itself, a final checklist of tips to follow, which, if ignored, can throw everything off.

By being aware of these details and knowing how to manage them, you will be giving yourself the last-minute support you need to:

a. make sure all the preparations and practice you've been through in the previous chapters aren't for naught.
b. push your speech, presentation, or interview over the top.

1.   Develop a Warm-up Routine

Warming up for stressful occasions, like public speaking or a job interview, is a good idea. It helps you release some of your nervous energy so that you don't get too wound up. And it helps put your voice and body in tune with each other.

I have a warm-up routine that I go through whenever I have a workshop or public speaking engagement. It's flexible enough for me to be able to do anywhere—at home, in my office, or in my hotel room—no matter how busy my schedule may be.

- 15 minutes of physical exercise
- 15 minutes of meditation
- 5 minutes of just talking out loud; I may even throw in a tongue twister or two

Just before I go on, I spend a few minutes alone to gather my thoughts. Some speakers like to mingle with their audience beforehand as a way of loosening up, and that's a good warm-up routine, too. I may mingle as well, but I will always create an opportunity to go off by myself and get focused just before I speak.

I cannot tell you what will work for you—only you know that. Some people tell me they jog, do yoga exercises, shadowbox, or dance wildly to loud music. Work up your own routine. Think of it as another tool, one that you can use as much or as little as you need, to get all systems going and moving in the right direction so that you hit the ground running and are off to a great start!

Taking It up a Notch

My good friend Marta Sanders is an award-winning cabaret singer and Broadway actress in New York City. Her advice is to "stand tall"—literally!—before going on. She says she takes a deep breath and stretches her body as high as it will go prior to making her entrance onstage, because she believes entrances and exits are as important as what happens in between. She maintains that standing tall improves her posture and boosts her confidence, and that it also leaves her feeling proud that she has been given the privilege to do what she does before an audience. This winning trifecta of good posture, a great attitude, and gratitude toward her audience gets her off to a terrific start, she says. Try it yourself prior to your next performance situation.

2. Watch What You Eat!

Avoid the following before your event:

Caffeine. Limit your caffeine intake prior to speaking. Beverages with caffeine, like coffee, not only make your throat dry but rev you up with all that high octane at the very time when your adrenaline is already making your head spin. If you absolutely, positively, no-way-nohow can't go without that cup of coffee to get you going, make it a decaf—or give yourself plenty of time before the event to absorb the caffeine into your system.

▌ *Eating too close to showtime.* You must eat to keep up strength, of course, but doing it just before you give your speech or sit down to be interviewed will have the opposite effect by making you feel lethargic and off your game. Eat well ahead of time, and give yourself plenty of time to digest your meal properly.

▌ *Sugar.* Replace sugary foods with protein items that will keep your blood sugar even and your energy high.

▌ *Dairy products.* They produce mucus, which interferes with speaking by making you cough, clear your throat, etc. Non-carbonated water at room temperature is the choice of professional speakers to keep the throat moist. Apple slices are also good for keeping the throat clear.

▌ *Alcohol.* Keep away from it. It wreaks havoc with your ability to add PEP (see chapter 7) by interfering with your articulation of consonants and vowels, and also slows down your pace and overall reaction time. Consuming alcohol prior to the event may make *you* feel relaxed, but in the end it makes your audience feel nervous!

3.   Dress Appropriately and *Comfortably*

The old adage "You can't judge a book by its cover" may be true, but it is also true that people do make snap decisions about our level of education, our background, our level of expertise and professionalism based on, among other things, how we dress. Though unrelated to public speaking, here is a nevertheless telling example of what I mean:

On a trip to Palm Beach with my husband, I inadvertently picked up the wrong luggage at the airport. It looked exactly like mine, and being in a hurry, I made the mistake of not checking the tags.

When we arrived at the hotel, I proceeded to unpack. I opened the suitcase and instead of seeing my clothes, I saw a man's! I looked on the bag for a nametag but there wasn't any. After we called the airline to report the error, my husband and I decided, with reticence, to search through the clothing to see if there was any identification inside.

As we sifted through the items without luck, we became curious about the owner and tried to determine what type of person he was based on his clothing. Here were some of our snap judgments:

▌ Three shirts, ties, and a jacket from Macy's, all with worn threading—not wealthy.

▌ Three pens in the jacket pocket—car salesman? Claims adjuster?

▌ An out-of-date brown leather winter-weight jacket, mid thigh—a fifty-something detective, maybe?

▌ No shoes—probably wearing his only pair and went straight to a meeting from the airport with plans to check into his hotel room later.

We really thought we had him pegged!

Early the next morning, the airline called and said, "Good news. We've got the man with your bag on the other phone." We were glad, of course, to hear that I would be getting my suitcase and clothes back, but also excited, because we would soon find out if our picture of the mystery man was accurate.

We were connected with him, told him where we were, and in a foreign accent, he said he wasn't far from us and would drive right over to exchange bags. So that I would be able to recognize him, I asked what kind of car he would be driving. "A white Mercedes," he told me, immediately altering my picture of him from that of a car salesman or claims adjuster to a high-profile lawyer . . . or a highly paid bookie!

We were waiting outside the hotel for him when he pulled up in his white Mercedes. The man with the accent who got out and greeted us was a nice-looking gentleman in his late fifties with graying hair. He had just come from the hospital, he told us, wearing a white lab coat with a stethoscope hanging from his neck. He was a doctor! Boy, had we missed the mark! All our assumptions were dead wrong! We had a good laugh.

There is no question, however, that in a business setting, your manner of dress says a lot about who you are, and, fairly or unfairly, audiences make interpretations. Take your image seriously by paying close attention to how you dress, so that the choices you make reflect the image you want to project.

Physical discomfort contributes to anxiety. There's nothing worse, for example, than wearing new clothes that don't fit comfortably yet to a speech or interview, or a too-snug new pair of shoes that raise blisters on your feet halfway through your presentation. I once saw a speaker walk up to the podium in a jacket so tight that it popped a button as she started to speak!

Wear clothing that fits comfortably and that you're not breaking in for the occasion. Tried and true is best. Similarly, wear a tried-and-true pair of comfortable shoes. They can be stylish, but make sure they're functional and you can walk in them!

4. Leave Your Personal Baggage at the Door

Although I addressed this issue earlier, it is worth raising it again here, because the experiences or situations that shape the mood we're in as we arrive for our speech, presentation, or interview occur nine times out of ten just before we get there. They can be a late plane, a suicidal cab ride, an emergency cell-phone call from home or work about a problem you can do nothing about, or whatever—and, presto, you're ticked off, frazzled, or upset. This is *so* common!

Professional speakers know—and know *how*—to deal with this. They go where they can be quiet for a brief moment, take a deep breath, and shift their focus where it belongs: on their audience and its concerns. Then they are able to deliver their speech, make that presentation, or breeze through that job interview as if nothing had happened.

If you're ticked off or frazzled when you arrive and carry that emotion into the room with you, no one but you will know why you are ticked off or frazzled, and no one but you will care. All your audience will be aware of is that a negative burst of energy has entered the arena, and things don't look promising. Like professional speakers, you must be able to shift gears, setting aside whatever personal tumult you may be feeling, and redirect your attention to your audience, almost on a dime!

One of the most compelling examples of this was a speaker I know who was scheduled to give a seminar on sales strategies a couple of days after the horrific events of 9/11. He did a wonderful job, according to everyone who attended. Nobody knew that his brother, a New York City firefighter, was counted among the missing in the fallen World Trade Center. Quite obviously he was upset about this, not knowing whether his brother would be found alive or dead, so I later asked him, point blank, how he was able to go on with the show under such devastating personal circumstances. What he said to me was this: "When I fly somewhere, I don't want to know whether the pilot's having a bad day. His job is to get me there safely, and that's all I care about. The same is true of me. I am being paid to show up and help people do what they need to do better, and sharing my problems won't help them do that."

I was very moved by what he said. He raises the bar for all of us, professional public speakers and inexperienced beginners alike!

5. Keep It Light—and Keep It Going

As I've written elsewhere in the book, we all make mistakes, or something goes wrong, during showtime, no matter how well prepared we are. Let me reiterate: it's not the mistake but the recovery that counts. If you maintain your grace under pressure (through proper breathing and other techniques I've shown you) and keep your sense of humor, you can turn any "disaster" to your advantage, just the way professional speakers do.

For example, a client of mine, a dentist, was nervous about a speech he had to give at his local dentists' association. He had worked hard and was well prepared. He energetically made his way to the lectern and accidentally hit the microphone with his arm, sending a loud *scre-e-e-c-h-i-n-g* sound through the room that deafened everyone. He was mortified, but as the noise subsided and everyone started getting their hearing back, he looked at the audience with a grin and quipped into the microphone, "Oops, I guess the Valium just kicked in."

Everyone laughed, which made him relax, and he went on to give a successful performance as a result of how he had handled that stressful gaffe.

You are human, and the audience is rooting for you. If you make a mistake, or something goes wrong, your listeners' initial reaction isn't to lynch you but to think, "Yikes! That could be me up there!" If you handle the situation well, they will, too.

6.   Be Prepared to Solve on-the-Spot Problems

For example, many people today are using laptop computers in conjunction with their speeches or presentations. In fact, as a video support tool for such events, laptops are becoming the business and industrywide standard. Projected on a big screen, the video and other graphics of a laptop can look great and add tremendous oomph to your performance. But while laptops provide many great options to public speakers and communicators, a lot of things can go wrong when using them—and do, typically at the worst possible time. So, be prepared to solve these problems on the spot. Here's how:

Bring Extras with You

In the case of computer equipment such as laptops, make sure to take along these extras:

1. Long AC extension cords so you can reach distant electrical outlets.
2. An AC multioutlet surge-protection strip, to enable you to plug all electrical equipment (laptop, video projector, microphone) into one source.
3. An AC 3-to-2 ground lift adapter. This is a very important extra in case you find yourself in an older building that has 2-prong instead of 3-prong AC outlets.
4. All necessary cables to connect your laptop to your video projector.
5. Black gaffer's tape (made by 3M), to tape down wires so that neither you nor anyone else trips.
6. Most important, a fully charged spare battery for your laptop (though always run off the AC power adaptor rather than battery when possible).

Have a Backup Plan

In the event that the whole system crashes or there is a glitch, a backup plan will save the day.

1. Make sure the battery in your computer (and the spare you've brought along) is fully charged in the event there is an electrical power failure.
2. Provide handouts to your audience. This way, you can say, "We are experiencing technical difficulties," ask the audience to refer to your handouts, and keep going. I saw this happen to a professional speaker recently. He was making a presentation using PowerPoint when the video projector went on the blink. He stopped and said, "Okay, if you just look at page 4

in your handouts" and continued seamlessly. Your handouts serve as a nice "takeaway" for your audience, as well.

7.   Add Professional Touches That Build Confidence, Enhance Credibility

To play a sport you need the right gear—the best helmet for safety; a fast bike built to last; the best-fitting, most durable sneaker for your foot; etc. All of these accoutrements are needed to increase your chances of success because they boost your confidence.

The same is true of public speaking. You need the proper gear, those professional touches that will make you feel and look confident, enhance your credibility, and ensure your success.

For example, if you will be speaking or presenting from a podium or in a large auditorium, unless you have the lung power of an opera star, you will likely want to use a microphone—but you will also want the freedom to move about so that you can get closer to your audience and maintain eye contact.

Some venues may not have microphones that will allow this (or the right ones *for you*), so I suggest that you invest in a wireless radio lavaliere microphone of your own—especially if you will be doing a lot of public speaking or presenting in the future. You can purchase one made by such reputable manufacturers as Shure, Sennheiser, Sony, Telex, or Vega, to name a few, at a relatively low cost, from any large electronics or audio equipment store. In this way you will be totally free from having to worry about what microphone system (if any) the venue has available, and the more familiar you become with your own microphone (or any other equipment of your own), the more confident you will feel and the better you will perform.

As you gain more experience speaking or presenting, and become even more confident and adventurous, you can accessorize more and not be dependent at all on what technical equipment may or may not be available to you at the location.

👍🏻

Taking It up a Notch

Many speakers, especially executives and other business people, use a teleprompter to read their speech or other material. It allows them to look as if they are always maintaining eye contact with their audience even though their words are flashing in front of them. TV news anchors use teleprompters also, for the same reason. If you've never actually seen the device, what it basically does is run your notes or the script of your speech across a camera lens, which reproduces the text in large type. The reproduced text then scrolls along a line-of-sight screen between you and your audience at a coordinated pace that allows you to read comfortably. If you find that you will be using a teleprompter for your speech or presentation, make sure you schedule some rehearsal time with the machine's operator in advance. You will need it so that the operator can get used to your tempo and scroll your text in sync. That way, you and the operator won't get too far ahead or fall too far behind each other, and you'll come across naturally.

███

Do It Often!

Speaking is something you must do frequently, so that, as with any other skill, you will become more proficient at it over time. Conversely, the less you do of it, the rustier you will get.

Taking It up a Notch

If you will be working from a script or substantial out-line, a wonderful tool I recommend is the ScriptMaster portfolio made by Brewer-Cantelmo, Inc. It's a leather-bound carrying case for your scripts, outlines, or notes that looks attractive and neat when closed, and when opened, gives you tremendous flexibility turning pages or shifting them without losing your place, while maintaining good solid eye contact with your audience. It really helps give you that professional edge.

I recently saw a discussion between the actor Peter Falk (of *Columbo* fame) and a group of his fellow actors that addressed this point well, albeit in different terms. The question was posed to Falk whether he preferred working on the stage or in film. He said he liked both, but they were very different—that working on the stage was something an actor had to do often in order to stay in shape. In other words, film and TV actors have a hard time onstage if they have been away from it too long. The physical skill required is more demanding, Falk said, because acting onstage is "BIG." People come to the theater to see characters larger than life, and the actors must be able to meet that requirement physically, regardless of how tall or short, fat or thin they are personally, whereas acting on film and television is "SMALL," requiring more subtlety to keep the performance real.

In public speaking situations, you are not required to inhabit another character. The character is you. You are required to be your authentic self, but with more energy than you would exhibit, say, sitting around with your friends. Achieving this requires physical skill. The more opportunities you take advantage of to speak in new and different situations, the more proficient you will become at this skill—and the more fun you will have from now on speaking without fear, at last.

So, as they say in the theater: "Break a leg!"

It's showtime.

INDEX